FIT DOG

FIT DOG

TIPS & TRICKS to Give Your Pet a LONGER, HEALTHIER, HAPPIER Life

Arden Moore

FIREFLY BOOKS

A Firefly Book

Published by Firefly Books Ltd. 2015

Copyright © 2015 Quid Publishing

First printing

Publisher Cataloging-in-Publication Data (U.S.)

A CIP record for this title is available from the Library of Congress

Library and Archives Canada Cataloging in Publication

A CIP record for this title is available from Library and Archives Canada

Published in the United States by
Firefly Books (U.S.) Inc.
P.O. Box 1338, Ellicott Station
Buffalo, New York 14205

Published in Canada by
Firefly Books Ltd.
50 Staples Avenue, Unit 1
Richmond Hill, Ontario L4B 0A7

Cover and interior design: Clare Barber

Printed in China

Conceived, designed, and produced by
Quid Publishing
Level 4, Sheridan House
114 Western Road
Hove BN3 1DD
England

I dedicate this book to my sweet canine duo,
Chipper and Cleo; our favorite
"K9 cousins" Gracie, Maddie, Jeanne, Stan and
Buddy; and to the dogs all over the globe who
unleash joy and laughter in our lives.

Contents

Foreword 9

Introduction 10

Further Reading 186

Index 188

Picture Credits 192

Foreword

Welcome to *Fit Dog*. I'm sure you're going to find these pages incredibly useful throughout your dog's life. Whether you adopted a new puppy, have an adult dog, or are living with a canine senior citizen, you'll find information in these pages that will help you keep your dog healthy.

As a practicing veterinarian, I can vouch for the fact that how you care for your dog has a great deal to do with the length and quality of your pet's life. As a pet owner, it becomes important to educate yourself on the needs of your pet. Nobody is better suited to help you do that than the author of this book, Arden Moore.

Arden is experienced in all things dog. Her knowledge and talents in passing on that knowledge will prove to be helpful to you in keeping your own dog healthy and happy.

Within these pages, you'll find basic information as well as more advanced, detailed instruction. You'll find out how to groom and care for your dog's hygiene needs, how to train your dog the right way, when to take your dog to the veterinarian and what to expect when you do, and how to look after your dog in the event of an accident through the use of properly applied first-aid techniques. You'll also find out a bit about your pet's breed as well as other breeds you may be interested in knowing more about. There's all that and much more here.

So, read on and enjoy. I suggest you keep this book handy for future reference as well. This is the type of resource you'll want to refer to over and over again.

Sincerely,

LORIE HUSTON

LORIE HUSTON, DVM

Lorie is a Certified Veterinary Journalist. She was a 2014 Pet Industry Woman of the Year Award Finalist, and is the author of *Labrador Retrievers: How to Be Your Dog's Best Friend* and the founder of Pet Health Care Gazette and Social Media Savvy Pets.

Introduction

Think of this book as your customized guide to all things D.O.G! It is filled with step-by-step guidelines, tips and tricks and insights—all designed to ensure your canine chum enjoys a long, healthy and enjoyable life.

Sure, cats may outnumber dogs in households all over the planet, but dogs still hold the acknowledgment of being man's (and woman's) best friend. Canine popularity is stronger than ever. Face it, our dogs definitely influence us in what we buy, what activities we do, where we live and how we decorate our homes. I readily admit that I bought my home because it had a fenced backyard and space for me to construct an enclosed canine condo on the side of my house with a doggy door from my living room. I was never big into running races until I had the opportunity to participate in "5-K9" races—that is, 5-kilometer (3-mile) races with people running with their leashed dogs. Walk into my home and you will find pet-friendly flooring: tile and laminate—two surfaces far easier to clean up doggy accidents than thick carpeting.

Paw through the pages of this book to discover such things as how to outsmart your misbehaving dog by re-channeling his need to dig or chew in more acceptable ways. Find out how to stretch your family budget without sacrificing the quality of care for your dog, as well as basic first aid for your pet. And learn how to make smart nutritional choices and prevent your dog from turning into an overweight chowhound.

I am honored to be your guide for you and your 21st century dog. Ever since I was a toddler, I've shared my life with a dog or two. My canine friendship began with a sweet, slightly overweight Beagle named Crackers and a spirited Border Collie mix named Peppy, who joined me swimming at our backyard lake and sharing spots on my bed at night. My current dogs answer to the names Chipper and Cleo. At age 11, Chipper, a Siberian Husky-Golden Retriever mix, maintains her youthful energy and outlook on life. Named for my love of golf, Chipper is a second-chance dog turned canine celebrity, appearing on numerous television shows with me and assisting me in my hands-on pet first-aid classes. Cleo, a Miniature Poodle-Basset Hound mix, was rescued as a scared stray and now lives for warming laps and, when the weather is right, surfing. She landed in the Guinness World Records as one of 17 dogs to ride into shore on one surfboard. Now 12, we teasingly refer to her as the "Betty White of K9 Surfers."

Our canines have us at bark.
They delight us. They fascinate us.
They love us. So, it's time to call your dog over, dive into these pages and learn how to truly be your dog's best friend.

Arden Moore

CHAPTER 1
General
Health

How Healthy is Your Dog?

One of the best ways to be your dog's best friend is to tap into all your senses in inspecting her. Special training is not required—you just need observational skills and a commitment to your dog's health.

How well do you really know your dog, from head to tail? An annual veterinarian examination is a must for every dog, but it is only the starting point in looking after your dog's health. Your mission is to identify what is normal for her and be able to catch early warning signs of trouble before they become major health concerns. That means looking, touching, smelling.

Instead of mindlessly patting your dog on the top of her head, start petting her with a healthy purpose. Once a week, pick a quiet time away from distractions and devote 5 to 10 minutes to inspecting your dog from nose to tail. These weekly at-home health checks can pick up on potential problems early, when treatment is more effective. Recognize what is normal and healthy for your dog, and pay attention to any changes. Don't forget that changes in your dog's routine—how much she eats or drinks, her elimination schedule, when and how long she sleeps and her energy level—can be indications that she isn't feeling her fit canine self.

Here are 10 at-home health checks for you to perform that are fast, easy and effective. Jot down the vital signs and record any changes so that you can report them to your veterinarian. Let's start with a close-up inspection of your dog's head.

1 CHECK YOUR DOG'S EYES.

Healthy eyes are bright, with no signs of any red or yellow tinge to the white of the eye (also known as the sclera), or the lining of the eye. The pupils should be symmetrical and should quickly constrict to a bright light and grow larger in a dark room. There should not be any discharge (mucus) oozing from the tear ducts.

2 CHECK YOUR DOG'S EARS.

Your dog is blessed with keen hearing. Whether your dog has erect ears or flop-down ones, she has the muscle ability to pivot each ear independently and zero in on sounds from varying distances and volume levels. Inspect the outer and inner ear for any signs of redness, scrapes, excessive wax or smell. A dog suffering with ear mites, for example, will have what looks like coffee grounds inside the ear.

3 CHECK YOUR DOG'S NOSE.

A healthy canine nose may be black, pink or spotted, depending on the breed. Any nasal discharge should be clear and not in excessive amounts. Contrary to what you may have heard, a healthy nose can be wet or dry. But it should never be extremely dry and cracked or extremely moist with thick mucus.

4 CHECK YOUR DOG'S GUMS AND TEETH.

Most dogs sport pink gums, a sure sign of health. Gently open your dog's mouth and assess her gum condition. This is called the capillary refill test (CRT). Take your finger and gently press and release against the gum above one of her large canine teeth. If circulation is healthy, the color should return to pink within 2 seconds. Next, inspect your dog's 42 teeth for any signs of missing or cracked teeth and finally, take a whiff. You should not be able to detect any "doggy odor" breath. Foul-smelling breath could be a sign of periodontal disease or an ailing organ, such as the liver or kidneys.

5 CHECK YOUR DOG'S RESPIRATORY RATE.

Count the number of breaths your dog takes per minute. Make sure she is at rest when you do this. Each respiration equals one inhalation and one exhalation (look for the chest to rise and fall). A panting dog—one who is cooling down from a game of fetch or back from a brisk walk with you, for example—will breathe more rapidly than normal. When your dog is at rest, her breathing should be even and regular, not labored. The breaths per minute should be between 10 and 35 (see box).

6 CHECK YOUR DOG'S HEART RATE (PULSE RATE).

With your dog standing, press your open palm against the rib cage over the heart and count how many heartbeats you feel per minute. Or get your dog to lie down on her side and gently press your two middle fingers on the inner side of her hind leg, toward the groin to feel for the femoral artery. Count the beats for 1 minute. In large breeds, the beats-per-minute range is 60 to 100 and in small breeds, the range is 100 to 140 (see box).

7 CHECK YOUR DOG'S HYDRATION.

Gently lift some of your dog's skin from the back of her neck and release. The skin should spring back immediately. If it does, this means that your dog's skin has good elasticity and serves as a sign that she is getting enough fluids and is not dehydrated. Another sign of dehydration is sticky gums. A hydrated dog displays wet-to-the-touch gums.

8 CHECK YOUR DOG'S COAT AND BELLY.

Glide your open palm down your dog's body from the base of the tail to the head and then gently in the other direction to lift the coat hair. Do you see any small dark brown or black spots on your dog's body? These may be fleas, and they can make your canine miserable. Matted hair can also be painful and lead to skin irritations. Examine for any bumps around the spine and palpate the abdomen to feel for any lumps or skin tags or signs of discomfort.

9 CHECK YOUR DOG'S TAIL AREA.

The canine tail contains numerous tiny bones. Dogs use their tail for balance and to convey moods. Gently glide your hand on your dog's tail and look for any cuts, bumps or bald spots. Inspect her anal area, checking for any swelling, redness or oozing.

10 CHECK YOUR DOG'S PAWS.

With your dog sitting or lying down, lift up each paw. Inspect the paw pads for any cuts or cracks or redness. Make sure each nail is not too long or curving and don't forget the dewclaws, which are located on the inside of each front paw. If the claws are too long and curving, it's nail-trimming time to stop them from getting stuck into carpet.

HEART AND RESPIRATORY RATES

A healthy dog's heart rate range is based on beats per minute and the size of the dog. The rate for large dogs ranges between 60 and 100 beats and for small dogs, between 100 and 140 beats. For puppies under 1 year of age, it is between 60 and 220 beats. Stress and diseases (including cardiomyopathy and Cushing's disease) can cause elevated rates.

A healthy dog's resting breathing rate ranges between 10 and 35 breaths per minute (count the chest rise and fall).

Try this simple counting method to save time. Instead of timing the rates for a full 60 seconds, simply count the beats out loud for 15 seconds and then multiply by 4.

Visiting the Veterinarian

Book your canine in for a thorough wellness veterinary examination at least once a year. Twice a year is even better to ensure any conditions are picked up early when treatment can be most effective and costs less.

For your dog's sake, take on a very special new role of pet detective. Your mission is to gather as many clues as possible to determine if a visit to the veterinary clinic is warranted—or if you should monitor your dog at home for a day or so.

Emergency Situations

Here are dire health emergencies that demand contacting your veterinarian immediately and rushing your dog to the clinic:

- You cannot find a pulse or heartbeat in your unconscious dog.
- Your dog is having severe difficulties breathing.
- Your dog's gums are white or bluish (healthy gums are bubble gum pink).
- Your dog fell and broke her leg.
- Your dog is spurting bright red blood, possibly indicating a severed artery.
- Your dog was hit by a vehicle.
- Your dog was bitten by a snake or poisonous spider or stung on the face by bees or wasps and has labored breathing.
- Your dog fell from a balcony or open window two stories or higher.
- Your dog suffered bite wounds in a fight with another animal.

- Your dog's eye is protruding out of its socket or is enlarged. Or you notice one eye is fully dilated and the other is not, suggesting a neurological condition.
- Your male dog is straining to urinate and crying, indicating a blockage.
- Your dog strikes her head hard or has a seizure.
- Your dog suffers second- or third-degree burns on her body.
- Your dog has a fever with an elevated temperature above 104°F (40°C).
- Your dog staggers, walks in circles and tilts her head to one side, indicating a neurological condition.
- Your dog has detectable blood in a runny or soft stool.

Situations to Monitor

Some signs are not so dire, but still merit a call to your veterinarian, who will decide if you should bring in your dog immediately or monitor your dog and bring her in the next day:

- Your dog begins coughing or sneezing constantly.
- Your dog has experienced diarrhea or vomiting for more than 24 hours and acts lethargic.
- Your dog starts drinking water excessively.

- Your dog's eyes are cloudy or she starts to squint.
- Your dog has a rash and is persistently scratching or chewing at her body.
- Your dog sports an unusual lump that is red, painful to the touch and warm.
- Your dog has a bloody nose.
- Your dog declines two meals in a day.
- Your dog starts drooling.
- Your dog has been limping for a day, but is still bearing weight on the leg.

Other General Health Issues

Finally, here are some less obvious indications that your dog may not be feeling completely well and require you to observe for a couple days or so and report your findings to your veterinarian:

- Your dog, who always alerts you when she needs to go outside to go to the bathroom, is now occasionally urinating or defecating inside the house.
- You notice that you need to refill her water bowl more often (a possible indication of diabetes).
- Your dog has lost a lot of weight in a month.
- Your usually perky adult dog is sleeping more and displaying disinterest in playing favorite games, like fetching or tug-of-war.
- Your dog's once-clear eyes are now weepy with excessive discharge from the eyes and even from the nose.
- Your dog's coat has become dry or matted or oily and smelly.
- Your once-mellow dog is suddenly full of energy, begging for food and losing weight.

CHECKING YOUR DOG'S TEMPERATURE

For dogs, a healthy temperature ranges between 100°F and 102.5°F (37.9°C to 39.2°C). To record your dog's temperature, gently insert a digital pet thermometer (lubricated with petroleum jelly) into the rectum. Another option is to use an ear thermometer that works by measuring infrared heat waves emitting from the ear drum. Place the thermometer deep into the horizontal ear canal to get a decent reading.

Take your dog to your veterinarian if her body temperature is less than 99°F or above 104°F (or below 37.2°C and above 40°C).

Work closely with your veterinarian to make sure that your dog is healing at a good progressive rate.

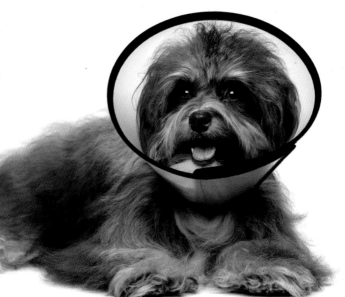

Work With Your Veterinarian

By working in harmony with your veterinarian, your dog stands a better chance of being diagnosed and treated more quickly and more effectively. And, as a bonus, you may be able to save on your veterinary bill.

After all, unlike your family physician, veterinarians face a special challenge: their patients can't talk to them or tell them where they hurt or how they feel. That's why providing specific info to your veterinarian during the visit is so crucial. Your details can help your veterinarian narrow down the possible reasons behind why your dog is ailing. Follow this handy checklist to maximize your next veterinary visit—for your dog's sake!

One way to keep close tabs on your dog's health is to book wellness veterinary examinations every 6 months.

Keep in mind that one of your dog's best health advocates should be her veterinarian.

BEFORE YOUR VISIT TO THE CLINIC
GET THE APPOINTMENT TIME RIGHT.
Strive to pick the first appointment of the day, if possible, or the first appointment after lunch to avoid waiting delays in the lobby.

ALLOW FOR TRAVEL TIME.
Give yourself a time cushion for unexpected traffic delays to ensure you arrive at the clinic on time. Show up at least 10 minutes early to fill out any necessary paperwork. Make sure your dog is secured inside a carrier or on a leash (ideally attached to a harness for more control) before exiting your home and entering the car to prevent escapes. Be sure the carrier is secured to your vehicle's seat belt in the middle seats—or for large breeds, the seat belt is fitted through a slot in the harness—for her protection.

BRING OUT THE CARRIER.
If you take your dog to the veterinarian in a carrier, bring it out the night before, open the door and pop in a tasty treat for her to find and enjoy. Some dogs dash away when you bring out the carrier because they equate it with riding in a car and heading to the clinic. This strategy will make the carrier less threatening.

COMPILE A LIST OF QUESTIONS.
Don't try to rely on your memory while you are in the exam room. Instead, bring a list of questions you want your veterinarian to address about the care of your dog. Ask about your dog's diet, bathroom habits, hair coat quality and other issues of concern. Finally, check in advance whether your veterinarian needs you to bring a fresh stool sample sealed in a plastic bag.

NOTE DOWN FEEDING HABITS.
Bring a list of the specific brand of food your dog eats, the exact amount you feed her daily as well as any treats she eats. If you can bring the bag that contains the list of ingredients, that's even better. Don't forget to note all medications, herbs and vitamin supplements that your dog takes.

CHART ANY HEALTH ISSUE.
Write down in advance all the "clues" you've detected about the change in your dog's behavior. For example, record the date when she started vomiting, having diarrhea, or started to urinate in the house. Name the time when your dog's appetite started to wane or accelerate.

AT THE CLINIC
TURN OFF YOUR CELL PHONE.
Practice phone-off etiquette in the exam room so that you can focus fully on your dog's examination.

USE A TOWEL FROM HOME.
Place a bath towel you have brought from home on the stainless steel examination table to make it more comfortable for your small dog to be examined.

SPEAK UP.
Be your dog's health advocate by discussing your concerns with your veterinarian. Write down the answers. However, when your veterinarian is performing a physical exam, especially when listening to your dog's heart and lungs, resist engaging in small talk so your veterinarian can get a good reading on your dog's vital signs.

ASK FOR HELP.
If your dog needs to be given medication at home (pills, liquid or injections), ask the vet staff to show you in the exam room the best medicine-giving technique.

SEEK TREATMENT OPTIONS.
Discuss cost and possible medication side effects before deciding on the best care option for your dog. And, inquire about any possible free medication samples that may be available to save you on your veterinary bill.

PLAY IT SAFE.
Before exiting the exam room, make sure your dog is leashed or safely secured inside her carrier so that she doesn't escape in the lobby or worse, dash out the clinic's door.

Your dog's health recovery depends on you making sure she receives all of her take-home medications as prescribed.

BOOKING A HOUSE CALL

Dogs need and deserve to be examined at least once a year by a veterinarian. But that doesn't mean that they have to be put in carriers, shuttled in vehicles and examined at a veterinary clinic. Consider making an appointment with a veterinarian who makes house calls if:

🦴 You have a dog who gets so stressed outside the comforts of your home that she urinates, defecates and/or vomits during transport. Why put her through this unnecessary stress?

🦴 Your dog behaves sweetly at home but transforms into a mean, angry canine who growls, lunges and attempts to bite inside a veterinary exam room. Such behavior prevents a veterinarian from doing a thorough examination.

🦴 You have several pets and want to avoid the logistical nightmare of booking multiple appointments to provide them routine care.

🦴 You have a dog who is in fragile health. She may be terminally ill or very old.

🦴 You don't drive.

🦴 You are in ill health.

🦴 You desire more personal care for your pet. A house-call veterinarian can see firsthand how your home environment may play a part in your dog's health condition.

🦴 Many procedures performed at a veterinary clinic can be performed in your home by a house call veterinarian. Physical examinations, blood and urine collection for lab work, vaccinations, microchipping for identification purposes, administering subcutaneous fluids, trimming nails and cleaning ears are among the services that can be performed by a veterinarian in your home. However, surgical procedures and taking X-rays must be undertaken at a veterinary clinic.

Medicine Time

Thanks to advances in veterinary medicine, dogs are living longer and healthier lives. But you play a key role in this by committing to giving your dog her prescription as directed.

Before reaching for the medicine bottle, put yourself in the right frame of mind. Be patient but purposeful because your dog can read—and respond to—your emotional state. Sure, the idea of trying to force a pill into your dog's mouth is not always comfortable for either you or your dog. Some dogs are difficult to "pill" because they don't like being restrained or having their mouth opened or the pill does not taste good to them.

When giving a pill to your dog, be confident and be quick so it does not become a struggle between you and your dog.

Pill-Giving Guide

In a technique known as counterconditioning, create a positive emotional state in your dog by first offering bite-sized treats. Consult your veterinarian in advance about hiding the pill in a soft piece of cheese or a commercial product known as a Pill Pocket.

1 Grasp your dog's upper jaw behind the canine teeth. If she wiggles or struggles, sit behind her or position her in a corner so that she can't back up.

2 Using your spare hand, hold the pill between your index finger and thumb. Place your third or fourth finger in the region of the lower incisors, avoiding the canines.

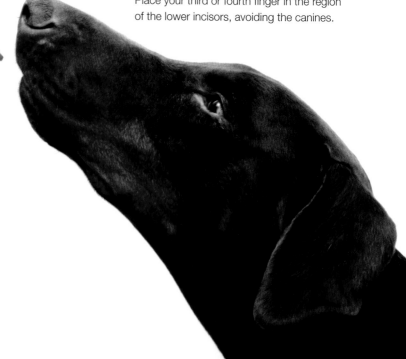

3 Open your dog's mouth and place the pill at the base of her tongue before she has an opportunity to resist. Avoid tilting her head because that can inhibit swallowing.

4 Close your dog's mouth and rub her throat in a downward stroking motion to encourage swallowing. You can also blow on her nose or cover her nostrils for a few seconds. Wait to release your hands until she swallows.

5 Follow with treats or water to ensure that the pill doesn't get stuck in the esophagus.

Liquid Medicine Guide

If your dog needs liquid medicine, make sure you know the right dosage to avoid an accidental overdose. Ask the veterinarian to mark the syringe to identify the amount using a permanent marker or tape. Once home, your goal is to get your dog to associate the syringe with a reward. You do this by dabbing canned cheese, peanut butter or other tasty treat on the outside of the syringe for her to lick. Praise her as she does this.

1 Put a small amount of the canned cheese or peanut butter on the outside of the syringe filled with medicine. The treat of choice won't mask the taste, but it will help to put your dog in a cooperative state of mind.

2 Keep her from wiggling free by positioning her body against you. This also prevents her from backing up. Restrain her head with one hand in a U-hold. With the treat on it and the medication inside, insert the syringe into the side of her mouth.

MEDICINE-GIVING OPTIONS

Consult your veterinarian about seeing if the three-times-a-day dose can be converted to one-time a day, or if you can split the pill for easier swallowing, use a pill gun, or pulverize it without compromising the effectiveness of the medicine.

The bottom line is your dog needs medicine and needs you to comply with your veterinarian's instructions. Your canine chum is counting on you to return to a healthy state.

3 As your dog focuses on licking the treat, inject the medication slowly into the back of her throat. Remove the syringe and close her mouth so that she can't spit out the medication.

4 As soon as she swallows the medicine, follow up immediately with a small healthy treat to reinforce medicine-giving time as a positive experience.

5 Clean the inside and outside of the syringe carefully before you put it away. Remember, it is important to take the time to train your dog that getting medicine is a fun procedure that merits tasty rewards.

CHAPTER 2

Knowing Your Dog

Doggie Communication

Got a case of canine confusion and frustration?
Here are reliable ways to converse effectively with your dog.

Canines communicate primarily through body language. Dogs don't deserve to be solely on the receiving end of one-sided conversations. They deserve to "speak up" to convey their wants, needs and feelings, too. The best way to engage in a meaningful two-way "conversation" with your dog is to speak less and stop, look and listen to what your dog is trying to tell you. Equally important is to look at your whole dog and assess the environment and situation. And remember, the best communication always involves sharing and receiving. That's the definition of a real conversation. So, how well do you speak dog?

Wagging Tail as You Approach
SCENARIO:
Don't assume that a wagging tail conveys a happy, friendly dog. Stop and look more closely. Is the tail making a circular movement or a stiff side-to-side wag? Or is the tail tucked between the back legs?

MOTIVATION:
Look at the tail in terms of the entire context of the dog's body. If the dog's body is loose, his eyes soft and the tail is mid-elevation, he can be happy or submissive, and it is safe to go slowly forward to greet. But if the tail is stiff, the body is tense, and the eyes are staring hard at you, these are warning signs not to approach.

SOLUTION:
You have to pay attention to the end of the dog that can really hurt you—the front end with the big teeth. When approaching a strange dog, don't be one of these three types of people: the clueless, the caretaker or the controller.

THE CLUELESS mindlessly approaches the dog head on.

THE CARETAKER assumes the dog is likely to be scared and needs to be comforted.

THE CONTROLLER believes they can overpower the dog with stern talk.

Leaping Up to Greet
SCENARIO:
It may have been cute when your 10 lb (4.5 kg) Labrador Retriever puppy rushed to greet houseguests by leaping on their legs. But now your dog weighs 90 lb (40 kg) and behaves more like a bruising linebacker toward your guests.

MOTIVATION:
From your dog's perspective, flinging his body at guests is a display of friendly affection. His goal is to get as close to the person's face as possible— and to try to lick it as a greeting. This behavior is unintentionally rewarded when the guest begins yelling or waving her hands in protest.

SOLUTION:
Nip this leaping habit early on by teaching your dog to obey the "off" and "sit" commands when guests arrive. When your dog stops trying to jump up and sits down, mark that desired behavior by saying, "Good sit" and giving him a treat. Also consider training your dog to do a polite paw shake or run to a designated spot like a rug for a treat when guests arrive.

Ignoring a dog's warnings can result in being bitten. So, take the time to properly read—and respect—the body posture a dog is delivering.

Doing the Hangdog When You Get Angry
SCENARIO:

You arrive home to discover a piddle on your new carpet or your lovely seat cushions shredded. You scowl at your dog with a cold stare and may even yell at him in your frustration. He responds by lowering his head, tucking his tail, and perhaps shaking behind the sofa. You convince yourself that your dog feels remorse for these misdeeds but this is in fact wrong.

MOTIVATION:

This hangdog look is not a guilty look, but rather a submissive posture from your dog with the purpose to turn off your aggression and to avoid a fight. Your dog is doing everything he can to calm down the situation and to regain favor with the leader of the house—you.

SOLUTION:

Dogs who receive daily exercise and have toys that engage them mentally and physically are less apt to warp into destructive dogs. Punishment after the fact is ineffective. Also, house soiling can be a sign of a serious illness, such as a urinary tract infection, that needs veterinarian attention.

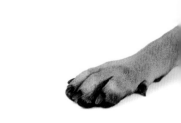

One of the most common misinterpretations of a cowering dog is that he is feeling guilty. More accurately, he is showing submissiveness to you.

Tilting Head Toward You
MOTIVATION:
Without a yap, your dog can indicate that he is fully focused on you. He may also discover that this action will garner him sweet coos and tasty treats from you. In essence, he has trained you.

Your dog may also tilt his head to attempt to tune into a strange noise in order to pinpoint its identity and location. Be aware though, that head tilting may be due to a medical issue that warrants veterinary care, such as ear infections, a burr lodged in the ear canal, or a head injury.

Barking Rapidly When the Doorbell Rings
SCENARIO:
The doorbell rings and your dog gets vocal.

MOTIVATION:
Quick "woo-woo" barks are the canine equivalent of sounding the alarm. Some dogs possess a natural distrust of strangers, especially those who dare to come into their territory. Most dogs want jobs and this style of barking is designed to earn their keep by defending the home turf.

SOLUTION:
Unfortunately, this barking escalates when we "bark" back by yelling at them to quiet down. Your dog interprets this as you are joining him in the barking chorus. Instead, acknowledge his detection by calmly saying, "I've got it. Go to your spot." In training sessions, use food treats to reward him for heeding your cues and move away from the door or wait on a rug, so you can open the door without his interference.

Dogs pay very close attention to your body language as well as your speaking tone in order to comprehend what you are conveying to them.

Barking Basics

The canine vocabulary is certainly not as large as the human vocabulary. Dogs choose their barks, woofs and growls carefully. Listen carefully to truly understand what they are conveying to you.

Some dog breeds have reputations for being yappers (we hear you, Mr. Chihuahua and Ms. Schnauzer), whereas other breeds prefer to wag more and speak less, such as the Basenji and Afghan Hound. Although dogs prefer to "chat" with nonverbal body posturing, they definitely have a range of woofs that convey specific meanings based on the pitch, pace and overall tones. Let's run down the most common canine sounds directed at people.

Be careful not to mistakenly encourage your yapping dog to bark more by yelling at him to quiet down. Your canine thinks you are joining him in the bark sessions.

A succession of sharp barks could mean your dog is very bored or very frustrated.

SINGLE BARK OR TWO

This is a need-to-find-out-more-information vocalization. Your dog is stating, "Hey, I'm here! What are you doing?"

REPETITIVE BARKS

Listening to the "bark-bark-bark" feels like a broken record. Nonstop barking often signals sheer boredom in a dog that is home alone or canine frustration that he is not able to clearly convey to you what he wants.

GROWLING

The growl does not always mean "back off." Growls come in different durations and pitches. A confident dog telling you to move away will deliver a low-pitched growl. Meanwhile, a scared dog who really doesn't want to defend himself may emit a high-pitched growl-bark to attempt to get you to move away from him.

HOWLING

Certain breeds, like the Siberian Husky, arch their heads up and let loose with this elongated musical note. Dogs howl to alert other members of the pack out of view of a possible danger or if they are in pain.

WHINING

Look closely and you will notice that a whining dog always makes this high-pitched sound with his mouth closed. This is definitely a canine call for help and/or for attention.

Canine Moods

For the most part, dogs love to please their favorite people. But they are also candid in what they want and when they want it so being able to assess your dog's emotions is quite important.

In order to properly read your dog's mood, you need to consider the entire package, which includes body language, postures, vocalizations and actions. You also need to factor in the environment or situation to put all of these canine clues into context. Just like us, dogs feel joy, fear, pain and contentment. Here are primary canine emotions directed toward people.

Affection
WHAT TO LOOK FOR:
Dogs do have favorite people, including you. They convey this adoring emotion by delivering kisses to your face or hand, wagging their tails in a relaxed circular cadence, flipping over to expose their bellies, following you in a happy trot from room to room and greeting you when you enter the front door like you're a famous celebrity.

HOW TO RESPOND:
Greet your dog by saying his name in a friendly, upbeat tone. Treat your dog to 1-minute attention sessions in which you focus entirely on your dog and deliver purposeful pets from head to tail. Make him feel incredible and his loyalty and love for you will grow.

Anxiety (stress)
WHAT TO LOOK FOR:

When faced with circumstances beyond their control, anxious dogs tend to hide, vocalize, and even pant or whine. They may also display their fear by trembling, pacing, tucking their tails, avoiding eye contact, yawning, blinking excessively and clinging to a trusted person.

HOW TO RESPOND:

In extreme cases, a veterinarian may temporarily prescribe anti-anxiety medication coupled with behavior modification designed to make this anxious dog feel safer at home and outside. Avoid talking in cooing tones or baby talk, as this may cause your dog to feel more nervous and anxious. Cultivate a safe routine for your dog by teaching him to sit and stay in a designated spot and rewarding him with a healthy treat and gentle affection. Give him ample time to acclimatize to new family members or changes in the routine.

Aggression
WHAT TO LOOK FOR:

Aggression runs the gamut from being fear-related (protective of resources or territory) to pain-related (a medical condition or injury). A dog full of ire or in pain gives warning signals before lunging or biting. Look for a tensing of the muscles, forwarding or flattening of the ears, prolonged staring, upper lip lifting to reveal teeth, raised hair (hackles) on the spine and body leaning forward. In some instances, the dog will also snarl or growl.

HOW TO RESPOND:

Heed these warning signs and never approach a strange dog quickly. He is clearly conveying a "back off" message. If your normally sweet dog displays aggressive behavior at his food bowl or when chewing on a bone, he is exhibiting resource guarding that needs to be addressed with behavior modification techniques. Work with a professional dog trainer or behaviorist to correct this potentially dangerous behavior. Never physically hit an aggressive dog because such action may escalate this behavior and seriously impact your relationship, making him mistrust you.

Do not allow early signs of anxiety to go unchecked. Your dog could develop a serious condition that requires anti-anxiety medication.

🐾 Beware of the bored dog. He can quickly turn into a destructive dog.

Boredom
WHAT TO LOOK FOR:

Dogs lacking enough mental and physical stimulation will display their boredom often in unwanted and destructive ways. They may dig holes in the backyard, chew shoes, shred toilet paper or bark excessively among other ways to convey that they need something to do. Unchecked, bored dogs can become physically depressed.

HOW TO RESPOND:

Jazz up your dog's indoor environment with food puzzle toys that test his brain power and coordination to fish out pieces of kibble. Schedule mini play sessions every day with your dog. These sessions can be as short as 5 or 10 minutes, but both of you will reap plenty of benefits by spending quality time together. If your dog has a pile of toys in your house, leave some out and store the rest. Every few days, rotate a new set of toys to maintain your dog's interest in them. When departing your home, leave on the television so the home is not too quiet for your stay-home dog.

Curiosity
WHAT TO LOOK FOR:

These canines are adventure seekers who may put themselves in harm's way with a determination to investigate. They boldly explore their surroundings by tapping into all of their senses. Puppies and young adult dogs risk physical injuries by being daredevils who fail to assess the situation before chasing, leaping or other such actions.

HOW TO RESPOND:

Definitely pet-proof your home room by room to minimize the risk of injury toward your curious dog. That means putting sharp objects like scissors and sewing needles out of paw's reach, stabilizing shelves and keeping your dog out of the kitchen when you are cooking on a hot stove. Provide your curious dog with challenging games, such as finding the hidden treat stashed under one of three upside-down buckets or finding a family member in another room in a game of "I-hide-you-seek."

HOW SMART
IS YOUR DOG?

In the dog world, owners of so-called Einstein breeds (such as Poodles and Border Collies) like to explain how smart their dogs are by bragging how many human words they know and how quickly they can master complex requests, such as turning on a light switch or opening a refrigerator door to fetch a beverage. But there are other ways to test your dog's IQ. Try this:

1 Line up three empty plastic buckets on the floor. Turn them upside down.

2 Get your dog to sit in front of the buckets and make sure there are no other distractions in the room.

3 Hold up your dog's favorite treat in front of his face and then place it under one of the three buckets.

4 Distract your dog by telling him to stay and then walking behind him, asking him to heed the "watch me" cue. Do this for just a few seconds. You are intentionally testing his canine smarts by diverting his attention temporarily from the hidden treat.

5 Resume your position by the buckets and then ask him to find the hidden treat.

EXPLANATION:

Brainy dogs make beelines to the correct bucket, knock it over, and grab the treat in mere seconds. They possess the cognitive development to know to look behind—or underneath—a solid object to find the missing treat. Not so smart dogs may paw over the other two buckets first before finally realizing where the hidden treat really is.

Obsessive-Compulsion
WHAT TO LOOK FOR:

Dogs diagnosed with obsessive-compulsive behavior can display this neurological disorder in many different ways. Some may frantically pace back and forth. Others may engage in marathon barking for no apparent reason. Some may lick their paws or coats so excessively to the point of creating bald spots. Still others may repeatedly run in tight circles in a determined quest to catch their tails. These abnormal actions can increase to the point to put your dog in serious harm. Some obsessive-compulsive dogs can potentially harm other pets and people in the home.

HOW TO RESPOND:

Identify causes of environmental stress within your home by going room to room. Did you relocate furniture or welcome a new member to the family (person or pet)? Your goal is to break these bad habits by providing your dog with a predictable daily routine for feeding, playing and socializing. Resist laughing at your dog's odd antics because you will inadvertently motivate him to intensify these behaviors. Instead, interrupt your dog when he starts to chase his tail or other obsessive-compulsive actions and direct him to a more acceptable action such as practicing basic obedience cues like sit and come. In some cases, your veterinarian may need to prescribe behavior-modification medications.

Playfulness
(attention-seeking)
WHAT TO LOOK FOR:

Young, frisky dogs don't have a monopoly on play. Some senior dogs maintain their zest for taking brisk neighborhood walks, inviting you to play fetch (rolling the ball on the ground) and showing interest in learning new tricks. Play-seeking dogs of all ages may try to engage you by flopping on their sides and going belly-up or pawing your arm or leg. Or they may let out friendly, short yips or drop their favorite slobber-drenched toy in your lap. Some overly zealous playful dogs may not know how to control their exuberance and can accidentally injure you by leaping or clawing you during play.

HOW TO RESPOND:

First, embrace this spirited canine who regards you as a prime playmate. Play-minded dogs need and deserve mental and physical stimulation every day. Read out loud from your favorite book—these dogs don't care about any story plotline, they just want your attention. They are perfect candidates to learn cool canine tricks, such as sit, give me paw and sit up. Consider using clicker training techniques in teaching your dog new tricks. Don't ever forget to give lots of praise as these dogs thrive on applause.

It is tough to keep a straight face when your dog acts like a four-legged clown in hopes of garnering your attention but try not to reward any excessive, overactive behavior.

Predatory
WHAT TO LOOK FOR:

These dogs are hyped-up hunters focused on stalking, chasing and biting perceived prey. That prey can be a stuffed pet toy, a less-confident pet in your home, or a squirrel spotted during a leashed walk in the neighborhood. These dogs tend to display stares without blinking, ears that are upright and forward, and tense bodies crouched low and ready to lunge forward. Another key clue of a predatory dog is that they generally do not bark right before the chase because they do not want to alert their targeted prey.

HOW TO RESPOND:

Offer a suitable hunting experience by occasionally feeding kibble without a bowl at mealtime. Instead, encourage your prey-minded dog to hunt for pieces of food you strategically place in a room. On daily walks, refocus your dog's attention from potential prey (like squirrels in trees) to you by mixing up the pace of the walk, the route, and by keeping a bag of small treats with you that you dole out each time your dog performs a cue on command. When your dog starts displaying predatory signs, clap your hands to disrupt and then rechannel his attention to sit or stay or "watch me" cues and then treat or praise.

Submissiveness
WHAT TO LOOK FOR:

These dogs emit a woe-is-me look identifiable by crouching, licking their muzzles, avoiding direct eye contact, flattening their ears, emitting soft whimpers, and possibly, plopping down and going belly-up or even urinating a little during introductions with a person or a dog they perceive to be dominant or even aggressive. These dogs are trying to do everything they can to avoid a fight—be it a verbal or physical one. In essence, they slink up as if to say, "I come in peace."

HOW TO RESPOND:

Submissive dogs need your help to boost their confidence and to feel safe in any situation. Avoid talking baby talk to these dogs—or yelling at them in frustration—as both extreme emotions will only heighten their fearfulness. Instead, slowly build up your dog's confidence by patiently praising and rewarding him when he conquers small challenges—such as coming when called or finally climbing up stairs.

Most dogs do their best to convey respect to the leaders of their pack— usually you. That explains such submissive postures as going belly-up.

Popular Breeds

There seems to be more physical diversity among canines than most other types of species. Most cats are generally about the same size, but canine breeds vary in lots of ways. Make sure to choose the type for you.

According to the international registry association, there are about 170-plus distinct dog breeds ranging in size from under 3 lb (1.1 kg) to more than 200 lb (90.7 kg) and from nearly hairless to sporting a full, fluffy coat. Year after year, here are arguably the top five breeds in terms of popularity in ascending order.

5 Bulldog

APPEARANCE:

The family of bulldogs, from the American Bulldog to the French Bulldog, shares trademarked pushed-up snouts, barrel chests and stocky frames.

BRIEF HISTORY:

The pack of modern bulldogs hail from the mighty Mastiff breed, a large solid-built dog known for size and strength.

PERSONALITY:

There is good cause behind the phrase, "As stubborn as a bulldog." This breed puts the "D" in determination and needs to be well schooled in doggy obedience and be under the guidance of confident, caring pet parents. Bulldogs are strong yet possess a gentle, patient attitude toward their family, making them ideally suited for children.

PRIZE FACT:

The heavy girth of bulldogs make them stars on surfboards because they don't tend to fall off. (But these canine surfers must wear life jackets because they can't swim.)

4 Beagle

APPEARANCE:

This medium-sized breed sports droopy ears, a white-tipped tail, and a tricolored coat with spiky hair. This popular member of the hound family also comes in white-and-black and white-and-light-brown coats.

BRIEF HISTORY:

This hunting breed came upon the scene in the 1830s in Great Britain as the result of breeding various hounds. The Beagle was first recognized by the American Kennel Club in 1884.

PERSONALITY:

This scent hound possesses one of the most powerful noses of the canine world, making the Beagle a top candidate as a drug detection dog. This even-tempered breed loves being around people and is very social. Because Beagles are so scent-driven, they can be challenging to train to come on cue when off leash.

PRIZE FACT:

Beagles gained headline attention in the 1950s with the debut of the *Peanuts* comic strip by Charles Schulz, which featured the character Snoopy.

3 Golden Retriever

APPEARANCE:

This large breed with a long, wavy coat and ready grin comes in blonde, yellow or gold colors. Many goldens love water and possess a water-resistant top coat.

BRIEF HISTORY:

The Golden Retriever hails from Scotland in the mid-19th century and quickly gained in popularity for his wildfowl hunting prowess.

PERSONALITY:

Golden Retrievers tend to be smart, loyal and loving, making them ideal choices as family pets as well as service-certified dogs for people with physical and visual limitations. This breed loves to fetch and hates to be left alone. This versatile, likable breed also excels in field trials, hunting, and obedience competitions. Some can even surprise you by being big "talkers."

🏵 PRIZE FACT:

Golden Retrievers have landed starring roles in Hollywood, including the series of "Air Bud" movies and Shadow from the movie *Homeward Bound: The Incredible Journey*.

Goldens have remained a popular breed for decades due in part to their sweet temperaments.

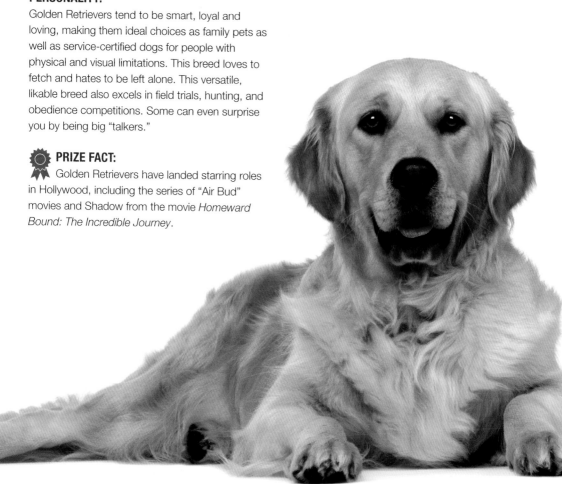

2 2. German Shepherd
APPEARANCE:

Big and muscular, the German Shepherd sports a black nose, long, square muzzle, upright ears, a bushy tail and a thick double coat. Popular colors are red and black or tan and black.

BRIEF HISTORY:

In 1899, a formal cavalry captain named Max von Stephanitz registered the first believed German Shepherd, named Horan, a result of breeding herding and farm dogs.

PERSONALITY:

Three words that best describe German Shepherds are "smart," "strong" and "protective." They need things to do because they possess plenty of energy. They want a purpose in life, which makes them ideal for military and police work and as service dogs for the blind and disabled.

🎖 PRIZE FACT:

The German Shepherd breed ranked No. 1 in popularity in America for most of the 1920s, but fell out of the top 10 ranking until after the end of World War II.

1 Labrador Retriever

APPEARANCE:

The perennial top dog globally, the Labrador Retriever is a large dog with floppy ears, and a short-coated, water-repellent coat in colors of yellow, black or chocolate.

BRIEF HISTORY:

The Labrador's birthplace is Newfoundland, where this breed came to be after folks in need of a dog to help with their fishing bred setters, spaniels and other retrievers.

PERSONALITY:

Labradors tend to grow physically faster than mentally and their high-excitability needs to be properly channeled early on. This eager-to-please breed thrives on learning and favors games of fetch and hide-and-seek.

🏅 PRIZE FACT:

Labrador retrievers are so adept at holding objects softly in their mouths that they can carry an egg without cracking its shell.

"Labs chew until they are 2 and shed until they are dead." This popular breed requires regular brushings to keep their coats looking shiny.

MOST POPULAR SMALL BREEDS

Depending on where you live, the reigning champion among tiny breeds is either the Yorkshire Terrier or the Chihuahua.

Posing cutely at 2 to 3 lb (1.1 kg), Yorkshire Terriers are can-do canines in tiny frames that love to learn and love to show off. Their silky, fine coat just begs to be stroked and they have mastered the art of tilting their heads to charm you into what they want—a treat, a lap, a car ride.

Small but mighty is the Chihuahua, a confident canine who weighs about 4 lb (1.8 kg). This breed comes in an abundance of colors and hair length and texture (from wiry or silky to single or double coat). The Chihuahua also enjoys one of the longest longevity among all dogs, averaging between 15 and 18 years.

Often sporting a reputation of being "small and mighty, and a little bit bitey," well-trained Chihuahuas can be very sweet to all they meet.

CHAPTER 3

Grooming and Hygiene

Why Groom?

Canine coats come in a variety of lengths and textures, from silky soft to wiry and even hairless. But no matter the coat, your dog needs you to keep her looking her very best year-round.

You don't want your dog to smell like, well, a dirty dog, or sport a shaggy, unkempt coat. Keeping your canine chum well groomed doesn't mean you need to obtain a degree in cosmetology or open your own pet salon. At-home grooming sessions can be a terrific boon to your friendship with your dog. With each session, you build up the level of trust. Take on the role as your dog's personal groomer and spend 5 to 20 minutes every day or week on grooming her. By investing this short time, you will reap these dividends:

- Your dog is less apt to contend with matted coats.
- You will be able to detect the presence of fleas, which can transmit disease, such as tapeworms.
- You can find suspicious rashes, lumps, bumps and other skin-related conditions at the onset, possibly saving on expensive veterinary bills.
- Your dog's claws won't become overgrown, causing them to snag or get stuck in the carpet.
- Your dog's breath will be fresh and her gums will be a healthy pink color.

One of the best reasons to groom your dog regularly is the ability to keep her coat free of any mats.

Seasonal Skin Care

When winter delivers its snowy punch, your dog must contend against two flakes: the snowy type and the dry, itchy type. Blame a dog's far-from-luster coat on exposure to temperature extremes of the blustery outdoors and warm indoors. Dogs with noticeably dry skin in the winter are usually the ones who nap next to a wood-burning fireplace or an air vent blowing out hot, dry heat. As a result, the skin becomes flaky and the coat has a dry feel to it.

Heed these at-home tips to moisturize your dog's coat and skin during the cold winter months:

PREP YOUR DOG'S COAT IN THE EARLY FALL.

Consult your veterinarian about adding a human-grade-quality food supplement such as Lipiderm, which contains omega-3 and omega-6 fatty acids, to your dog's diet. These supplements can add oil to a dog's skin and coat from the inside out. They often take 4 to 6 weeks to become effective, so don't wait until the heart of winter.

MAINTAIN A REGULAR BRUSHING SCHEDULE.

The brushing, combing action helps distribute a dog's natural oils and lift and remove dry, dead, flaky skin.

SELECT A MOISTURIZING PET SHAMPOO.

At bath time, make sure you use a pet shampoo containing a moisturizer. Allow the shampoo to sit in and absorb into the coat and skin before rinsing thoroughly. Don't use a shampoo made for people because it tends to dry out a dog's coat. Thoroughly dry your dog's coat before allowing her to go outdoors.

DON'T SKIP HAIRCUTS IN COLD MONTHS.

If your dog requires hair trims every 4 to 6 weeks, stick with that schedule, even in the winter. Just have the groomer use a longer blade. Skipping sessions during the winter months can cause your dog's coat to become matted and stay damp.

LIMIT YOUR DOG'S INDOOR ATTIRE.

Constantly wearing a sweater indoors does not allow a dog's skin to breathe, potentially causing dryness and flakes.

KEEP YOUR HUMIDIFIER HUMMING.

Remove static electricity in the air and add moisture by using humidifiers, especially if you have electric heat or burn fires in fireplaces. Provide warm, cozy dog beds away from air vents and fireplaces.

Hair Care

All dogs, regardless of breed, need to be brushed regularly by their owners. That even includes Great Danes! The key behind this "coat maintenance" is selecting the right brush and comb to fit the canine coat.

First things first, it is essential to use the correct brush or combs for your breed of dog. Select slick bristle brushes for smooth-coated and shorthaired dogs such as Beagles and Doberman Pinschers. For longhaired, thick-coated dogs such as Poodles and Yorkshire Terriers, use slicker brushes, pin brushes and wide-toothed Poodle combs.

Grooming Guidelines

Dogs seem to know that you are making them feel better when you treat them to regular grooming sessions. Once you've got the right tool or tools, follow this hair-care advice:

ADD GROOMING TO YOUR SCHEDULE.

Keep your dog's brush handy—perhaps in the living room—and brush your dog while you're relaxing or watching a television show. Use this time to look over your dog for any signs of fleas, lumps or bumps.

If you are unsure about the right brush to use on your dog, please consult a local professional pet groomer.

MAKE GROOMING SESSIONS SHORT.

A dog's skin is durable—it is thicker than a cat's skin—but it can still be irritated due to overzealous grooming sessions. Because of this, never comb one spot 1 minute or longer, because it can cause that area to become bald. You'll end up stripping out the good fur with the loose, dead hair.

GROOM IN THE DIRECTION OF THE LAYER OF THE HAIR.

Always brush or comb in the direction that the fur grows: from the back of the head to the tail. For the hips and shoulders, the hair grows straight down, so brush or comb downward. The hair on the tail grows sideways at a 90° angle, so brush or comb the tail outward at an angle from the base.

AVOID TENDER AREAS.

Work from the skin out and brush in the direction of the hair growth. Do not brush obvious tender areas like around the genitals, anus and eyes.

RECOGNIZE THE NEED TO BRUSH REGULARLY.

Remove the dead hairs underneath to clear the follicles for new healthy hair to grow in their places. Regularly brushed hair will not attract as much dirt.

BRUSH BEFORE BATHING.

It is important to remove all tangles, matted fur, and any foreign materials in your dog's coat before you wet the coat.

USE GLOVES.

One-size-fits-all grooming gloves quickly remove dirt, dust and dead hair from your dog's coat and are terrific for in between longer grooming sessions and when you want to have your dog look spiffy for houseguests. Or for quick grooming solutions, rub your dog's coat with pet wipes that reduce dander. Select brands that contain aloe vera or vitamin E to keep your canine's coat soft and shiny.

BATTLE EMBEDDED PET HAIR WITH BALLOONS.

Ever try to retrieve short spiky pet hair from your sofa or car upholstery? Running a sticky tape roller brush over the surface doesn't always do the trick. Try this: fill a balloon, seal it and rub the balloon over the surface to create static electricity. This causes the embedded hair to pop up, making it easier to vacuum away.

TEST OUT DOG CLOTHES.

You don't have to create a new closet just for your pet, but having your dog wear a pet jacket or sweater in the house can keep their excess hair under wraps—literally. Less hair will shed onto your bedspread or sofa. Just make sure that the indoor temperature is cool enough for your pet to sport her jacket.

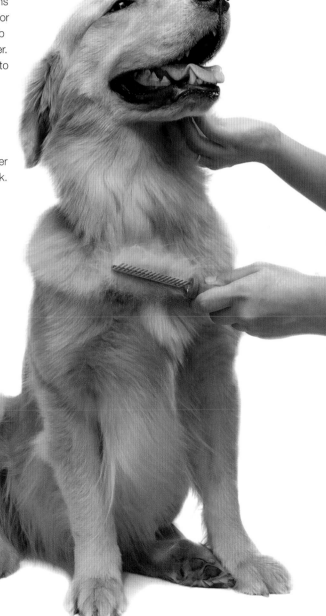

Brushing Wiry Coats

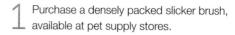 Love your terrier but frustrated when it comes to keeping her wiry coat in tiptop shape? Among the popular breeds that sport wiry coats include Scottish Terriers, Affenpinschers, Otterhounds, and there is even a wirehaired variety of Dachshunds. In between appointments with a professional groomer, consider these tactics to tackle this type of coat:

1 Purchase a densely packed slicker brush, available at pet supply stores.

2 Coat your fingertips with resinous chalky material to allow you to grasp the dead hair in need of removal. Or place rubber thimbles over the fingertips (the same item used to help turn a book's page).

3 Place your dog on a moistened bath mat on a counter or table waist-high to you. The mat provides sure footing for your dog.

4 Rake your fingertips through your dog's coat, starting from the shoulders and moving along the back toward the tail.

5 Run the slicker brush from the shoulders to the back to gently but firmly pull out dead hair. Liken this movement to typing on a keyboard, pressing one letter at a time, or eating an ear of corn.

6 After the brushing, bathe your dog in cool water with antibacterial soap. Rinse thoroughly. Cool water helps close the pores, a much better choice than hot water, which can inflame or irritate the skin.

7 Finish with brushing the coat in the direction that the coat grows. Never brush against the grain.

Brushing Double Coats

Double-coated breeds, including Collies, Samoyeds, Keeshonds, Elkhounds and others, typically sport a silky topcoat and a coarse undercoat. Depending on the climate where you live, your dog's breed and health, you can expect her to "blow her coat" once or twice yearly—heaping piles of dead hair all over your home—unless you invest 10 to 15 minutes three times a week in brushing your dog.

Regular brushing will remove dead hair, keep your dog's body oils in the coat for a nice texture, and your dog won't have as many skin problems, like flakiness or dander. For the hairy job, use a dog rake, brush (pin brush for Collies and slicker brush for Elkhounds), and comb from a pet supply store. Place sheets of newspaper on the ground or table to catch your dog's discarded hair and dander. Then follow these steps:

1 Rub a dab of mink oil or coat conditioner through your dog's coat. Both are available at a pet supply store. These oils work to remove tangles.

2 Rake through both coats in a head to tail direction. Go slowly to loosen up any snarls and pull hair underneath up and out.

3 Brush by lifting up the hair and brushing the underside. Be careful not to brush too harshly and irritate the skin.

4 Comb through to remove remaining dead hair. (A good idea is to collect all of the brushed hair clumps as you go to make disposing of it easier.)

5 Run a damp cloth over your dog's coat to pick up any dander. Finish with a bath, if necessary.

Dogs with double coats can be at risk for heat stroke in hot climates so keep them safe.

Icky Goo—What Do You Do?

Sometimes, dogs can be as curious as cats. In their adventures inside the home and out, their hair coats can pay the price. You look down and discover your dog's fluffy white tail sports splashes of baby blue paint you just applied to your bathroom wall. Or, your dog couldn't resist rolling in the just-paved road and brandishes patches of tar on its back. Or, returning from the hike in the woods, you notice burrs causing a tangled mess in your dog's chest hairs. When it comes to paint, tar and burrs, no need to throw in the towel. Help is here. Heed these effective at-home tips for three common coat problems.

BURRS

After each hike, inspect your dog's coat, paying close attention to the footpads and under the legs where burrs can harbor. Burrs are best removed on dry coats. Most can be removed by using your fingertips or tweezers in a sliding outward motion. Snip stubborn burrs with thinning scissors. The best preventive against burrs matting the fur is to brush your dog at least weekly, if not daily. Burrs and stickers tend to slide right out of regularly groomed coats.

STICKY TAR

Rub vegetable shortening, olive oil or mineral oil into the affected areas until the tar softens. Follow with a slicker brush. Do not bear down on the skin. Instead, pull outward to avoid causing a brush burn against the skin.

OIL-BASED PAINT

If the paint area is small, dampen a cotton ball with mild fingernail polish remover product and dab on the painted area. For large areas, wipe the fresh paint off with clean dry cloths by working on the ends of the hair and not rubbing inward (you risk getting the paint down to the skin). Then wash your dog's coat in warm water and pet shampoo. Once your dog's coat has completely dried, use clippers to cut off the remaining dried paint. Never cut below half-inch above the skin to avoid accidentally cutting into the skin. If you don't feel comfortable, make an appointment to have the paint snipped off by a professional groomer.

When you need to take on a home project such as painting, keep your dog in an enclosed room while the walls dry or have someone treat him to a long walk.

DEALING WITH MATTED HAIR

Conquer mats in longhaired coats by brushing them daily using a wide-toothed comb. Start by carefully pulling apart the mat with your fingers as much as you can or use a mat-splitter. Holding the mat at the base, gently but firmly work out the mess with the comb by starting at the tip and working in toward the base. For any mats you cannot comb out on your own, please seek help from a professional dog groomer rather than removing it with scissors.

Never bathe a dog without first getting out all of the tangles. The tangles only tighten, worsening the situation. If your dog has mats, try using cornstarch. Simply sprinkle cornstarch on the mats to help loosen the hair. If necessary, cut away dense mats with a pair of blunt-tipped scissors. Be sure to cut away from the skin. Finish the grooming session by rubbing your dog's coat with a soft chamois cloth to add luster.

Bath Time

Even spelling out the word b-a-t-h can be enough to send some dirty dogs scampering far away from the bathtub or shower. With the right approach, you can make this necessity fun and inviting for your dog.

Some dogs take to water like, well, ducks. Others do everything they can to duck out of bath time. But baths are necessary. How often depends on your dog's coat—and her habits. If she likes to dive in mud puddles or chase after skunks or do full-body wiggles on dead fish, be prepared to spend more time bathing her.

Home Bathing Guidelines

Pick a time when you have time. Do not try to squeeze in a dog bath on a busy day. Never attempt to groom or bathe your dog when you are in a hurry or your dog is agitated. You risk escalating her stress level and upping her resistance. Make these at-home bathing sessions inviting for your dog and teach her that everything is okay. Stick to these steps to achieve bathing success:

PREP THE BATHING AREA.

Gather all your bathing supplies in advance and position them so that they are easily within your grasp in the bathroom. Make sure you have three towels (two for drying and one for her to grip), shampoo, brush, comb and treats. You don't want to be hunting for missing items after your dog is wet.

HAVE A LEASH AND A BATH TOWEL.

Keep your dog on a leash. Preferably nylon and not a leather one, which can shrink when wet. Have your dog sit on an old beach towel inside the sink or tub to prevent her from slipping too.

USE LUKEWARM WATER.

Temper the water temperature. Use lukewarm water from a gentle spray nozzle, if possible. The water should be a gentle spray against your dog's body and feel inviting, like a warm massage. Gradually, wet your dog, starting from the bottom up. Never spray water up in the nose or inside the ears.

AVOID GETTING SOAP IN YOUR DOG'S EYES.

Never use a spray nozzle to wet your dog's face. Instead, clean the face with a warm, wet washcloth with a dab of shampoo. And, if you do get soap accidentally in your dog's eyes? Rinse, rinse and rinse. Or, before the bath, take a little mineral oil and drop it in your dog's eyes to help protect her from soap.

NO NEED FOR COTTON SWABS INSIDE EARS.

Don't probe inside your dog's ears with cotton-tipped swabs because of the risk of accidentally poking and damaging the ear drum. Instead, clean inside the ears with cotton balls, but don't probe deeper than what you can see easily.

RINSE THOROUGHLY.

If you do not rinse completely, your dog can end up with skin issues. Wash off the shampoo effectively before drying. She may start to chew her coat and develop skin irritations. One way to tell if you have rinsed thoroughly is to bring your ear down to the coat and squeeze the wet hair. If you hear a squeaky clean sound, that means you have rinsed out all the shampoo.

DRY THOROUGHLY.

Allow your dog to shake off the excess water before toweling dry. Be gentle if you use a handheld blow dryer to avoid frightening your dog. Have two thick bath towels within reach. Towel dry your dog well with the first towel. Then snugly wrap your dog in the second towel and hold her closely. Speak sweetly to her to help her feel calm and secure. If you do use a hair dryer, brush the coat first and then only use the dryer at a low setting from a distance to avoid burning your dog's skin.

BUYING SHAMPOO

Purchase hypoallergenic shampoo. Avoid shampoos that contain artificial dyes, petrochemicals, parabens and sodium lauryl sulphate. For routine cleanings, use hypoallergenic, tear-free shampoo available at pet supply stores. You may need a special flea shampoo if your dog has been itching from these pests.

Bathing Hairless Breeds

Folks sharing their homes with hairless and near hairless breeds can rejoice about not having to clean up clumps of hair, but you shouldn't skimp on grooming sessions. Topping the list of popular "bald" breeds include American Hairless Terrier, the Chinese Crested, the Mexican Hairless and the Inca Hairless Dog (also known as the Peruvian Inca Orchid). In addition, other popular dogs, such as the Dachshund, feature single-coated, short-cropped hair.

These dogs need to be bathed regularly, at least once a week. That's because their coats still produce natural oils that need to be kept in good condition. Their skin pores need to be free of clogs that cause doggy odor. If you need a visual, think of their skin like your own. You wouldn't consider going 2 months without washing your hands, would you? Choose shampoo and conditioners that are hypoallergenic and scent-free to prevent skin rashes.

The reality is that hairless breeds require more baths than dogs with double-haired coats.

Follow this step-by-step guide when bathing your dog:

1 Put equal amounts of shampoo and water in a bottle. (Remember to select gentle dog shampoos or diluted mild baby shampoos.)

2 Bathe your dog in tepid, not hot water. These dogs are very sensitive to hot or cold water, so make sure the water is slightly warm to your touch.

3 Blot your dog dry with a thick towel. Do not rub the towel on your dog's skin.

4 Keep your dog indoors in a warm place for about an hour after the bath to ensure its skin has completely dried. Skin holds moisture and your dog can get chilled if you let it outside right after a bath.

EXTRA CARE FOR HAIRLESS SKIN

Hairless breeds require a different type of care to short- or longhaired dogs. It is important to offer protection for your canine's sensitive skin.

🦴 Apply colorless, odorless, mild sunscreen products on your dog's coat. Dab a little on your hands and rub the lotion into the skin rather than misting the coat with a sunscreen spray. You risk missing some spots or putting too much sunscreen in other spots.

🦴 Clothe your dog in lightweight cotton T-shirts for protection in warm climates and doggie sweaters or coats in cold climates to keep its body temperature regulated properly.

Ear Care

Dogs can tune into more sounds at greater distances and wider frequencies than we can. It doesn't matter if your dog's ears are erect or folded, they are better than any human's and need regular cleaning.

Practice routine ear care at home and you can prevent a lot of ear woes in your dog. You may find the source behind that incessant scratching by looking inside your dog's ears, such as a buildup of gunk, dirt, wax or, worse, ear mites. Sniff your dog's ears at least monthly too, and if they emit a foul odor, consult your veterinarian.

Consider keeping commercial medicated ear powder and commercial ear-cleaning solution, both available from a pet supply store or drug store, at home. And mint-flavored mouthwash and white or apple cider vinegar are two surprisingly effective household products that keep canine ears clean and odor-free. The mouthwash is a great ear cleaner because the alcohol in it removes dirt, gunk and grease plus the mint makes the ears smell good. Vinegar offers an antibacterial, antiseptic effect to kill germs in the ears.

Never use cotton swaps in your dog's ears. You risk probing too deeply and damaging the ear canal.

Follow this step-by-step guide when cleaning
your dog's ears:

1 Lift your dog's ear flaps and remove as much hair
  as possible with your clean fingers.

2 Remove excess wax by spraying a light amount
  of medicated ear powder into the ear canal.

3 Saturate a cotton ball (with the ear- cleaning
  solution or mouthwash or vinegar) and use a twist-
  and-turn motion outwardly to scoop out gunk and
  wax and not drive the debris deeper in the ear canal.

4 Always make ear cleaning an upbeat event.
  Praise your well-mannered dog and offer
  a tasty treat after the chore is done.

CANINE HEARING

In general, dogs can hear between 67 and
45,000 Hertz (Hz), a measure of sound
frequency or cycles per second. By
comparison, people hear sounds in a
frequency range up to 20,000 Hz.

If your dog is starting to
scratch his ears often, it could
signal a possible ear infection
that needs veterinary care.

Nail Care

There are dogs who act like they are four-legged politicians—always ready to extend a front paw to greet. And, there are dogs who do not like having their paws touched. Both types rely on their nails to dig and get traction and depend on you to keep their nails healthy.

Dogs typically have five nails on each front paw and four nails on each back paw. These claws are curved and require the tips to be clipped every few weeks or so to prevent them from overgrowing and worse, growing back into the paw. Before your first nail session, play with your dog's feet regularly to get her used to you touching her toes. Gently squeeze her footpads to expose the nails and release. Pet her and give her a small healthy treat.

For dogs who love to greet people, train them to shake paws with the right one first and then the left one. It will be a time to show off their neatly kept nails.

Follow this step-by-step guide to clipping claws for a doggone great peticure:

1 Set out the tools you need: nail clippers designed for dogs, a thick towel, and styptic powder (just in case you clip the nail too short and it bleeds).

2 Wrap your small dog in a large bath towel, exposing one nail at a time to better handle her safely. (For a large dog, you could use a large bed blanket or bed spread as opposed to a towel. Muzzling is much easier on large dogs—unless, the dog has difficulty breathing due to an injury or illness.)

3 Position your thumb on top of one paw and your fingers of that hand underneath. Then gently press to expose the nail.

4 Snip the tip of the nail—the clear, white part. Do not cut too closely to the pink area of the nail (called the quick—the vein that runs through the nail) or it will bleed.

5 Keep styptic powder or cornstarch within reach just in case you do nick the quick to quickly stop the bleeding.

6 Heap on praise during and immediately after the trim session. You want your dog to have a positive experience.

Inspect your dog's nails on a regular basis to be able to prevent overgrown nails and to quickly treat any split nails.

Teeth and Gum Care

Canines can develop gum disease, plaque and calculus buildup, oral tumors, and even need tooth extractions. Maintain wellness examinations at your veterinarian clinic and regularly check your dog's teeth and gums.

It goes without saying that you love your dog and want her to be healthy and happy. But by age 3, nearly 75 percent of dogs develop some form of dental disease! Don't let your dog fall victim to periodontal disease. Maintain twice-a-year wellness examinations at your veterinarian clinic. Practice dental care tactics:

LOOK AND SNIFF.
Examine your dog's mouth daily. Report any swellings, bleeding or sores to your veterinarian promptly.

MONITOR MEALTIMES.
Dogs who eat slower than usual, suddenly spill kibble on the floor, or back away from the bowl may be experiencing oral pain.

DAILY BRUSHINGS.
Treat your dog to daily brushings —or, at a minimum, once a week.

SHOP SMARTLY.
Use only toothpaste approved for use on dogs—never human toothpaste (contains fluoride). Select products that bear the Veterinary Oral Health Council (VOHC) seal. Dog toothpaste should contain antimicrobial enzymes and come in a flavor your dog likes, such as chicken, seafood or beef.

Toothbrushing Guide

Angled toothbrushes with soft angled bristles make it easier to brush the exterior on either side of the mouth. Finger toothbrushes feature soft bristles and enable you to easily slide it between your dog's gums and cheek.

With your dog in a sit position, reach your arm around and approach her mouth from the side. In other words, never face her head on, or attempt to push a toothbrush straight into her mouth. This is a threatening position for dogs. Once you are in position, here is the recommended step-by-step guide to follow:

1 **MASSAGE AND RUB YOUR DOG'S CHEEKS.**
The idea is to get her used to you touching her face. Reward her with a small tasty treat. Do this briefly each day over several days or longer until your dog is clearly comfortable with it.

2 **INTRODUCE THE TASTE OF TOOTHPASTE.**
Place some toothpaste on the toothbrush and let her lick it off.Once she's accustomed to the "treat," slide the toothbrush inside the pocket between the outside gums and the inside of the cheek. Concentrate brushing on those outer surfaces. Don't forget to praise your dog and reward her afterward with her favorite treat.

3 **HOLD YOUR DOG'S HEAD IN YOUR LESS-DOMINANT HAND.**
Lift her upper lip with the same hand. Use your dominant hand to massage your dog's cheeks briefly then slip a finger into her mouth just a little. Give her a treat. Repeat daily.

4 **STRIVE FOR GAINING YOUR DOG'S TRUST**.
As tolerance builds up in succeeding daily sessions, gently use your finger to rub back and forth over the gum line. Start at the front of the mouth, and then move to the back upper and lower gum areas. The idea is to get her accustomed to having something in the mouth. Always reward.

5 **UP THE ANTE.**
Now that your dog accepts a finger in her mouth, you're ready to begin the hygiene session. Wrap gauze around your finger. With a circular motion, rub your dog's teeth and gums along the gum line. Try to apply some digital pressure to the teeth and gums. Usually, there is no need to open the dog's mouth into a gape—plaque is mostly accumulated on the cheek surfaces of the teeth. Always reward. Repeat over the course of days or weeks until she accepts this routine.

6 **TIME FOR THE TOOTHBRUSH.**
Hold the brush at a 45° angle to the gum line. Move it with an oval motion or brush back and forth. Start with the outer surfaces and possibly finish with the inner surfaces. That way, if your dog starts fussing and attempting to wiggle free, the most likely area of plaque accumulation has been brushed. Keep the session brief—just 1 minute or two. Reward with a treat.

ALTERNATIVE OPTIONS

If your dog won't tolerate you brushing her teeth, don't fret. You have other options, including the use of oral rinses, oral cleansing gels, dental gauze, water additives you add into your dog's water bowls and dental treats. Top-quality dental products feature anti-bacterial and odor-fighting properties.

CHAPTER 4
Food and Nutrition

Food for Thought

For our pets, mealtime and treat time are big deals. They depend on us to give them complete and balanced diets that keep them healthy.

Dogs are lousy spellers until you spell the word, "t-r-e-a-t." I'm betting that before you can finish the final "t," your dog is dashing into the kitchen and plopping into a polite sit to await a tasty reward and looking at you with those adorable begging eyes.

Food is vital. Food is powerful. Think of food as fuel. It's what keeps our pets' bodies humming. The right food in the right portion can fortify your pet against disease and keep his coat shiny. The wrong foods in the wrong portions can weaken your pet's immune system, cause intestinal upset and leave his coat dull or oily. It can also necessitate the need for more veterinary visits, costing you time and money. Maximizing the nutritional best in your pet goes beyond the food served. Frequency of meals, location, post-meal bowl cleaning and other factors impact the quality of your pet's health.

Let's start by defining dogs when it comes to nutrition. Dogs are obligate omnivores. That's a fancy description to declare that their bodies fare best with meats and plant substances. All dogs of all sizes sport digestive systems engineered to digest and absorb protein from plant sources as well as from meat. Their bodies benefit from being fortified by meats, fish, dairy, fruits, vegetables and grain products. Dogs depend on these six classes of nutrients for growth, maintenance and repair of skin tissue:

- Protein
- Fats
- Carbohydrates
- Vitamins
- Minerals
- Water

Feeding Time Guidelines

What is the best food to serve your pet? There is no one-answer-fits-all. There is no one magic commercial brand of food for all dogs. Selection should be based on your pet's age, breed, activity level and health condition. What you serve your 2-year-old, agility-competing Corgi will be different than what is best to serve your 12-year-old, sofa-lounging Labrador Retriever. Have a chat with your veterinarian once a year about what to feed your pet. Work together to identify a meal plan that is both balanced and appetizing for your dog. To make mealtime more satisfying and safe for your dog, factor in these environmental considerations:

RESIST BUYING GIGANTIC BAGS OF FOOD.

You will get more than you bargained for— increased risk of the food becoming stale and contaminated. Instead, buy about 1 month's worth of dry food and empty the food into a plastic container with a lid. Before refilling that container, always thoroughly clean it and allow it to air dry. The reason? Fats sprayed on the dry food leave a greasy film on the inside walls of the container, which can cause the new food to quickly become rancid.

SERVE UP TWO OR THREE MINI-MEALS A DAY.

In general, far too many dogs would eat, eat, eat until you intervene. They have a reputation for being gorgers, but you can maximize your dog's metabolism by feeding him two or three mini-meals a day rather than one big meal a day.

SEPARATE DOGS AT MEALTIMES.

This is especially relevant if you have a canine food bully or a dog on a therapeutic diet. Mealtimes should be calm, welcoming events so that dogs can properly digest their food. Stress created by other pets in the household trying to steal your dog's food can cause stress and, possibly, even gastrointestinal upset. Veterinarians recommend training the dogs to eat in separate rooms at mealtimes, where doors can be closed. Dogs like routine and, in time, they may even park themselves in front of their designated rooms at mealtime, waiting for you to feed them.

BRING OUT THE MEASURING CUPS.

Although suggested food portions are often put on the bags of commercial dry food and canned foods, measure your dog's meals precisely and work with your veterinarian on establishing the right daily portions to meet your dog's age, health condition and activity level. By knowing how much you are feeding, the portion can be adjusted if your veterinarian determines you are under-or-over feeding your dog.

SOAK AND CLEAN BOWLS.

Food bowls can be coated with salmonella in the bio-film. Water in bowls can get stale. Clean your dog's food bowls after each meal in hot soapy water and rinse thoroughly and allow to air dry. Do the same daily for his water bowls. And, don't forget to regularly clean your pet's measuring cup or serving scooper.

PAY HEED TO THE CONTENTS OF YOUR FLOOR-CLEANING PRODUCTS.

Many household cleaning products contain bleach, effective in killing viruses on the kitchen floor. However, dogs have sensitive noses and some may be repelled by the odor of cleaners. So, never clean your kitchen floors before mealtimes.

If you notice that your normally neat-eating dog is starting to spill kibble, it could mean that he is dealing with a toothache or gingivitis that needs veterinary care.

MONITORING WATER INTAKE

It can be challenging to make sure your dog laps up enough water each day to stay properly hydrated. Here are tips and tricks to follow to increase your dog's water intake:

🦴 Serve up canned food because it has more moisture than commercial dry food.

🦴 Add sodium-free broth to his dry food to make it more appealing to him.

🦴 Locate water bowls throughout the house so he doesn't have far to travel to find a watery oasis.

🦴 Add tuna juice to jazz up the taste of the water.

🦴 Provide a pet fountain that features moving water. Some dogs are attracted to flowing water. Avoid letting your faucet drip because you risk having a high water bill.

🐾 **Consider feeding your dog with an aluminum bowl with a nonslip bottom. The bowl is easy to clean and tends not to flip over at mealtime.**

SELECTING FOOD AND WATER BOWLS

The type of bowl you choose to fill with food or water does matter to your dog's health. Stainless steel or ceramic bowls are best because they are easy to clean thoroughly. Avoid plastic bowls. They can be easily nicked or chewed and thus create hidden havens for salmonella or other bacteria, causing digestive upset in your canine chum.

Once a week, purposely prepare a meal without the bowl. Bring out your dog's innate hunter by putting dry food in a food puzzle. His task is to lick, swat and nose out the pieces of kibble. Or, place a meal amount of kibble down a long hallway or on each step of a stairway. These are fun options that make mealtime more stimulating and include the opportunity to burn a few extra calories hunting for the food.

Purchasing Food

Face it, food is fuel for Fido. Invest in your dog's health by selecting a high-quality commercial food that meets your dog's specific age, breed, activity level and health condition.

 Step into any pet supply store, supermarket or even inside veterinary clinics and you can quickly become overwhelmed by all the choices of commercial dog food available. Interpreting canine food labels can prove to be a daunting task. To help you crack the commercial pet food code, abide by this handy checklist of do's and don'ts.

WHAT TO LOOK FOR
WHOLE PROTEIN AS THE FIRST INGREDIENT.

The ingredients are listed in order of weight, with the first one being the heaviest. Look for commercial diets that contain any of these highly digestible proteins as the first ingredient: chicken, beef, salmon, lamb, turkey. Avoid products listing "meat," "poultry" or "meat by-products" as the No. 1 ingredient. By-products can include feathers, feet, hooves, beaks and other unsavory body parts used in the processing. Really pay attention to the top five ingredients—they represent the majority of the ingredients contained in the commercial food. Skip products that list corn or wheat as one of the first three ingredients.

MANUFACTURER TRANSPARENCY.

A quality commercial food manufacturer makes it easy for the consumer to contact them by listing their website, consumer hotline phone number and where their products are made. They will also include an expiration date.

PROOF THAT THE FOOD IS COMPLETE AND BALANCED.

The label should confirm that the product is formulated to meet the nutritional levels established by a pet food monitoring agency, such as AAFCO (Association of American Feed Control Officials). If an over-the-counter food label states "for intermittent or supplemental use only," it is not complete and balanced and should not be fed on a permanent basis. Therapeutic diets prescribed by veterinarians may have this phrase when they are used to help manage medical conditions, but these special diets should always be fed under the supervision of a veterinarian.

A NUTRITIONAL LABEL FOR LIFE STAGES.

The life stages for canines include growth (puppy), adult maintenance, and reproduction (for pregnant and nursing mothers). Labels that state "all life stages" mean that the food has been formulated to meet the nutritional needs for a growing puppy, an adult dog, and a pregnant or nursing dog.

SHOP SMARTLY. Don't buy more than a month's worth of dry food. Store it in an airtight container to avoid it becoming stale or contaminated.

WHAT TO AVOID
PACKAGING STATING "HOLISTIC," "LITE," "PREMIUM" OR "ALL-NATURAL."

These are merely meaningless marketing terms designed to attract consumers and are not as the result of meeting any quality standard established within the pet food manufacturing industry or its monitoring agencies.

GRAIN-FREE COMMERCIAL DIETS ARE NOT ALWAYS FREE OF CARBOHYDRATES.

Even if the packaging claims to be "grain-free," look at the list of ingredients. Some brands are loaded with carbohydrates like potatoes or corn.

ARTIFICIAL COLORS, FLAVORS, SUGARS AND CHEMICAL PRESERVATIVES (SUCH AS BHA AND BHT).

Your dog deserves to eat healthy, clean food and not ingest potentially dangerous preservatives or chemicals in his diet.

CHOOSING CANNED FOOD OVER DRY FOOD BASED ON PERCENTAGE OF PROTEIN LISTED.

Be aware that the protein percentage in canned food is not on par with the protein percentage of dry food because canned food contains about 75 percent moisture as compared to dry food containing about 10 percent moisture. Comparing protein content from canned to dry can be confusing, so please ask your veterinarian for help.

MANUFACTURER DAILY FEEDING RECOMMENDATIONS.

These recommendations are coming from the manufacturer and may be more than your dog needs. Instead, work with your veterinarian to identify the right amount of food to feed your dog based on his age, health and activity level in order to keep him at a healthy weight.

Making Food

On special occasions, don an apron and treat your dog to a homemade nutritious meal. Here are three recipes that will evoke plenty of tail wags and drools from your dog. Bon appétit!

Mutt Meatballs
YOU WILL NEED:

1 lb ground beef or sirloin
⅔ cup grated cheddar cheese
2 carrots, finely chopped
1 cup breadcrumbs
6 tbsp tomato paste (low-sodium)

MAKES: *12 treat servings to a medium-sized dog*

1 Preheat the oven to 350°F [175°C].

2 Combine all the ingredients in a medium-sized bowl.

3 Scoop out by the spoonful and roll into mini-sized meatballs.

4 Place the meatballs on a cookie sheet sprayed with non-fat cooking spray.

5 Bake for 15 to 20 minutes.

6 Cool before serving and store the rest in the refrigerator in a container with a lid.

Chowhound Chicken Soup
YOU WILL NEED:

2 chicken breasts or thighs
5 cups water
2 large carrots, peeled and diced
1 celery stalk, chopped
2 potatoes, peeled and cubed
2 cups rice, uncooked

MAKES: *6 servings to a medium-sized dog*

1 Combine the chicken, water, carrots, celery and potatoes in a large pot.

2 Cover and simmer over low heat for 2 hours, stirring occasionally.

3 Add the rice and continue to simmer over low heat for 30 to 35 minutes, or until most of the liquid has been absorbed.

4 Remove from the stovetop and let the soup cool.

5 Pull the meat off the chicken bones. Put the meat back in the soup and toss the bones in the trash.

6 Stir the soup before serving.

7 Store leftovers in the refrigerator in an airtight container.

Tail-Wagging Turkey Pizza

YOU WILL NEED:

¼ cup turkey broth (low-sodium)
Pre-made pizza dough
1 cup diced cooked turkey
½ cup finely chopped spinach
1 cup grated mozzarella cheese
¼ cup sesame seeds

MAKES: *6 servings to a medium-sized dog*

1 Preheat the oven to 375°F [190°C].

2 Pour the turkey broth over the pizza dough.

3 Sprinkle the turkey, spinach, cheese and sesame seeds on top.

4 Place on a greased pizza sheet and bake for 12 to 15 minutes.

5 Enjoy your slice while it is warm, but let the slice for your dog cool before service.

HOME-COOKING HYGIENE

Keep your dog from stomach upset when making a homemade meal by always:

- Washing your hands in warm soapy water and rinsing before handling food.
- Trimming meats of fat and draining excess grease from cooked meats.
- Storing leftovers in airtight containers in the refrigerator.

The way to a dog's heart is through his stomach. On special occasions, display your devotion to your dog by creating a nutritious homemade meal or treat.

Treats

Did someone say treat? Arguably, the most treasured word to a dog is the word "treat." He is sitting pretty and giving you all his attention in hopes of reaping a lip-smacking reward.

Don't go hog wild on doling out the treats. The amount of treats should represent only 10 percent of your dog's daily nutritional needs, or about 20 to 25 calories. The majority of that food should be their regular kibble or canned dog food—not treats or table scraps. What your dog really wants is your attention. Engage him in a short play session. He will love the interaction with you and interaction is calorie free. Bring out your dog's innate hunter by making him work for his food by placing a daily portion of his kibble in treat balls that require him to swat to cause the kibble to fall onto the ground.

Treats to Avoid

Some dogs are fussy eaters whereas others behave more like chowhounds, quickly gobbling up any and all food opportunities. Veterinary nutritionists and toxicologists share this list of human foods and drinks to definitely never give to your dog:

RAW FISH OR MEAT

You may be a fan of the sushi bar at a Japanese restaurant, but don't give your dog any sushi leftovers or any uncooked fish or meat. Human-grade sushi is safe for people, but can cause gastrointestinal upset in dogs. Left unrefrigerated, raw fish or meat can contain bacteria, such as salmonella that can cause vomiting and diarrhea in your dog. In addition, an enzyme in raw fish can also destroy an essential B vitamin called thiamine that dogs needs.

UNCOOKED EGGS

Again, you risk exposing your dog to salmonella and other parasites that could cause vomiting, diarrhea, dehydration and possibly, pancreatitis.

FAT FROM MEATS

If you want your canine meat fan to enjoy a piece of your T-bone, cut a small lean piece and set it aside to give him as a reward for not begging. Do not give him the fat or grizzle from the steak. The fat can cause vomiting, diarrhea, and inflammation of the pancreas, leading to pancreatitis.

MILK

This dairy drink lands on the cautionary list. An occasional small amount of milk may be okay to some dogs, but keep in mind that a dog's digestive tract becomes somewhat lactose intolerant after puppyhood. Daily serving of milk can cause diarrhea and vomiting.

AVOCADOS

The biggest health danger to dogs is the persin found in the plant, leaves and fruit itself. Ingestion can cause vomiting and diarrhea in dogs.

ONIONS, CHIVES AND GARLIC

Dogs do not metabolize the alliums found in onions, chives and garlic as well as people do. These foods in any form (raw, powdered, cooked or dehydrated) can cause gastrointestinal upset and destruction of red blood cells, leading to Heinz anemia in some instances.

CAFFEINATED COFFEE, TEA AND SODA

Curious dogs may be drawn to lapping up your caffeine-loaded drink, but too much caffeine consumption can cause restlessness, heart palpitations, rapid breathing, muscle tremors and, possibly, seizures in your canine. Keep in mind that stimulant drinks such as Red Bull as well as some cold medicines and painkillers for humans also contain caffeine.

UNCOOKED BREAD DOUGH

Your placement of dough on a cookie sheet on your kitchen counter could spell an invitation to a food-seeking dog. Remember that the yeast in this dough rises. So, the dough can cause your dog's abdomen to swell and stretch, causing severe pain. The dough can ferment and expand in your dog's stomach, causing signs similar to drunkenness.

MACADAMIA NUTS

You may want to spoil yourself with these tasty and pricey nuts, but be aware that a dog who eats these types of nuts can choke, suffer vomiting and diarrhea, and, in some cases, even paralysis.

ALCOHOL

It only takes a small amount—2 teaspoons of whiskey—to damage your dog's liver, put him in a coma, or kill him. So keep all beer, wine and hard liquor out of access to your dog. A dog can get drunk, nauseous, and his respiration can be affected. A dog can aspirate vomit into his lungs. A dog can also injure himself because the alcohol has made him uncoordinated.

CHOCOLATE

We know this sweet treat is a dangerous temptation to dogs. Ingesting the ingredient, theobromine, found in chocolate can cause high heart rate, high blood pressure, tremors and seizures in a dog. The darker the color of the chocolate, the greater the danger to your dog's health. So keep your candies out of paw's reach.

SAFE FOODS

On occasion, it is okay to give your dog a little canned tuna, a tiny piece of your steak, or a small bit of cheese. But don't exceed your dog's daily caloric needs by going hog wild on these from-the-table treats.

Sizing Up Your Dog

Does your dog display more waddle than wiggle? Nearly half of the world's beloved pets are overweight or obese. Extra pounds in dogs hikes their risk for developing diabetes, respiratory and arthritic conditions. Sadly, these are often chronic, incurable and generally preventable diseases.

The root cause for pet obesity is guilt. Far too many people feel guilty that they live busy lives and don't have time to walk or exercise their pets, so they show their love by doling out too much food and too many treats. Pet obesity starts at the food bowl. To curb chowhound tendencies and shed excess pounds gradually but steadily off your dog, try these tactics:

SMILE, DOGGY.
Help your dog slim down smartly by taking a "before" photo of him and put this in a visible place. Start a food diary and weigh your dog once a week.

SET REALISTIC WEIGHT-LOSS GOALS.
It's best for a dog to lose only a few ounces per week (or 1 lb/0.5 kg or so for large breeds) so that the excess weight comes off gradually and doesn't return. Don't cut back too quickly. In dogs, the dangers of "crash dieting" can lead to hepatic lipidosis, commonly known as fatty liver disease.

COUNT THE KIBBLE.
Feeding as little as 10 extra pieces of kibble per day would add 1 lb (0.5 kg) of weight in a year in your small dog who weighs 10 lb (4.5 kg). So, use a measuring cup at mealtimes.

OPT FOR SCHEDULED FEEDINGS.
Instead of filling up your dog's bowl whenever it is empty, use a measuring cup and portion out your dog's daily meals twice a day. If you are unable to be home at a specific mealtime, consider buying a timed self-feeder that can dispense controlled portions of kibble at designated times.

CHAMPION THE CAN.
Canned food is what veterinarians regard as a close-calorie environment because you know precisely how many calories are in a can. Canned foods also tend to benefit dogs because of moisture content, higher fat and protein and lower carbohydrate content than found in some dry foods.

STICK WITH SIMPLE FOOD CHOICES.
When it comes to selecting healthy treats, look for ones with a single ingredient listed, such as sweet potato, blueberry, salmon flakes or dehydrated beef lung. If the label's list of ingredients reads like a chemistry equation, avoid this product. These treats contain additives, preservatives and way too many calories.

PLAY THE FIVE-QUESTION GAME WITH YOUR VETERINARIAN.
To keep tabs on your dog's health, ask your veterinarian these questions: What should I feed my pet? How much should I feed my pet? How much exercise does my pet need? What types of exercises are best for my pet? What vaccines does my pet need and why? Remember, for the health of your pet, you need an open relationship with your veterinarian.

ASSESSING CANINE
ADIPOSE TISSUE

Not sure if your dog is packing extra weight? You need to assess your dog by following these steps:

1 Stand in front of your standing dog. Exam his body profile. He should have a clearly defined abdomen slightly tucked up behind his rib cage.

2 Stand over your standing dog. Most healthy canines have an hourglass shape and you should be able to see his waist.

3 Gently run your fingers over your dog's backbone and spread your hands across his rib cage. You should be able to feel each rib.

THE RESULTS

OBESE DOGS: Fat deposits are readily visible on the neck, limbs, base of tail and spine.

OVERWEIGHT DOGS: The waist is barely visible and you can see fat deposits over the lumbar area and base of the tail. You can feel the ribs, but just barely.

FIT DOGS: You can feel the ribs without a lot of fat covering. Looking from the side, you can see the abdomen tucked up and you will see the hourglass shape when you look over your dog.

TOO-THIN DOGS: His ribs, pelvic bones and lumbar vertebrae protrude out and are highly visible.

Here is a clever trick to determine if your pug, bulldog or other barrel-chested dog is hefty or healthy:

- Glide the fingers of one hand over the back of your other hand. Feel the bones?
- Now, take your hand and glide over the base of your dog's back near his tail.
- Healthy dogs have that same bony feeling you identified in gliding your fingers over the back of your hand. Hefty dogs have a fat cushion that can be detected.

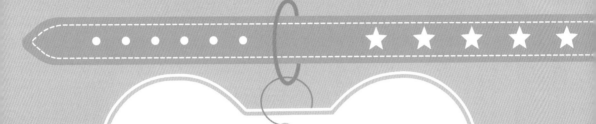

CHAPTER 5

Obedience Training

Obedience Training

Sit. Stay. Lie Down. Come. Good, doggy! What's the secret to training your dog to master these must-know cues? Two words: positive reinforcement.

Dogs, just like us, are more eager to learn when the teacher makes the lesson fun and engaging. Out with the word "No" and in with the word "Yes." Accentuate the positive when teaching your dog. No matter if you adopt a puppy or an adult dog from your local animal shelter, canine class should begin on Day 1. Here are three reasons why you should take the time to train your canine pal to heed these four vital obedience basics:

🐾 You can be a lifesaver. You can put the brakes on your dog darting out the front door heading toward traffic if she heeds your "come" cue by stopping and returning back to you.

🐾 You will earn your dog's trust and respect. She will want to please you by complying with your cues because she views you as the family's "top dog."

🐾 You create a foundation to enable your smart dog to learn other cues and even master some cool tricks.

Dogs learn best when you employ the three C's of canine training: be clear, concise and consistent.

Proper doggy etiquette is within your reach. It starts with proper training. Motivate with food lures and be consistent with voice commands and hand signals. You—and your dog—can be successful in mastering the basic cues with training strategies such as these:

AHEM: ATTENTION, PLEASE!
The only way to get your dog to successfully comply with your training is if you have her undivided attention. When you begin any training session, pick a place and a time where distractions are kept to a minimum. When you're ready, say your dog's name and wait for her eyes to meet yours. Clap your hands or whistle if you have to, but make sure she is watching you and waiting for her cue to see what to do next.

BE A LEADER, NOT A BULLY.
There is n need to shout or berate your dog. You will win her unconditional loyalty by being an effective teacher who relies on positive reinforcement techniques. Praise your dog's correct moves and ignore her mistakes during training sessions. Dogs learn by association and are apt to repeat an action when it is reinforced in a positive manner.

GIVE ME A C—FOR CONSISTENCY.
Decide on what verbal and physical cues you want for the must-know canine cues of "sit," "lie down," "stay," and "come." And then, stick with them. If you use the command "stay" in one training session and then "don't move" in the next, you will create canine confusion. If you're consistent with the cues, your dog will eventually catch on.

SPEAK PROPERLY.

When you teach your dog the essential basic cues, make sure the tenor of your voice is friendly, confident and encouraging. If you project frustration or impatience, those emotions can make it harder for your dog to learn.

STICK WITH TINY TREATS.

Training time should be a pleasant experience for your dog, so that's why using treats works. Keep those tasty tidbits tiny enough for your dog to bite once and swallow. By using small treats, you'll keep her attention on you rather than on causing her to be distracted by taking time to consume a large treat.

KEEP LESSONS BRIEF.

Dogs tend to learn better in training segments that are 10 minutes or less (unless you have an extremely focused, attentive dog). These mini training sessions also work better for you since they fit easily into your busy schedule. For example, you can squeeze in a short training lesson before you head off to work or when you get home after a long day.

THINK OF HITTING THE JACKPOT.

Slot machines do not deliver a payoff with each grab of the handle. If every time you played a slot machine it paid you exactly the amount you put in, you would quickly become bored and stop playing. Gamblers are attracted to slots because of the hope of hitting a jackpot. Psychologists call this "intermittent reinforcement." Apply this theory to training your canine student. Once you've taught the basics, bolster compliance by offering a treat intermittently. Keep your dog guessing about when she'll be rewarded—and how much—and she'll work harder for that tasty "jackpot."

VARY YOUR LOCALE.

Your canine may perfectly and quickly heed every cue inside your home, but misbehave and ignore you while at your local dog park. Set her up for success by first teaching her the basics in your home and then teaching her in various settings. This way, she understands that she needs to listen to you, no matter where the two of you are.

Sit
EASY ♪

GET READY: Regard the "sit" cue as the cornerstone to your dog's good behavior. After all, a dog in the "parked position" can't get into any mischief. Before you begin, break up semi-moist food treats into small, easy-to-swallow pieces and place in your pocket, a bait bag or on a table right next to you.

1 Get your dog to stand facing you.

2 Place bit of food between your thumb and forefinger and bring the treat to your dog's nose and get her attention with it. Let her lick or mouth at it, but do not give her the treat yet.

3 Slowly raise the lure up and as your dog follows it with her nose, move it back over her head a few inches. As her head tilts back, let gravity be your guide as the weight causes her to sit.

4 As soon as her rear touches the floor, say "yes" and give the treat. (If your dog jumps up for the treat, you may have raised the treat too high over his head. Keep the treat closer to her head when you try again. If she stands up or walks backward instead of sitting, try working in a corner with the dog against the wall when you try again.)

5 If your dog anticipates the next move and begins to sit before you move your hand up and back, she is ready to learn the verbal cue. Take a piece of food, hold it in your hand at about waist level, and when the dog looks like she's ready to offer the behavior, say "Sit." When she sits, say "Yes" and give her the food.

6 Practice with your dog both facing you and standing at your side. In order for her to really know the command, you must practice it in many locations, under various weather conditions, around different levels of distraction, and on different flooring surfaces.

Lie Down
EASY ♪
GET READY: Another key basic obedience cue for your dog to master is to lie down upon your verbal and hand signal cue. As with the "Sit" command preparations, put a handful of small tasty treats in your pocket or bait bag and sit or kneel on the floor next to your dog.

1 Tell your dog to sit.

2 Lightly rest your left hand on your dog's shoulders, but do not push down. This should help prevent your dog from standing up during the exercise.

3 Hold a small treat in your right hand between thumb and first two fingers. Allow your dog to nibble at the treat while slowly lowering it straight to the floor.

4 After your dog's nose has followed the treat to the floor, slowly drag the treat away from the dog, thus forming an "L" configuration. Most dogs will creep forward with their front legs to try to get the treat and lower themselves into a down in the process.

5 When her elbows and chest touch the floor, say "Yes" and reward with a treat.

6 After a few repetitions using only the lure to prompt your dog into a down, try introducing the command "Down" as her legs are stretched out and the chest heads to the floor. Reward when down has been completed.

7 Once your dog consistently lies down on command, practice on different surfaces, in different locations, around different levels of distraction, while giving the command from different postures (sitting, standing and lying down).

Stay
MEDIUM 🐾🐾

GET READY: Before introducing the "Stay" command, make sure that your dog consistently heeds the "sit" and "lie down" cues. Your goal is to teach your dog to stay put until you release her. Your mission with the "stay" cue is to gradually increase the time you want your dog to remain in one place, so you can build up trust between you and your dog as well as bolster her confidence. Don't expect your dog to sit for more than a few minutes the first few times you say, "Stay."

1   Get your dog to sit or lie down on your left side. Keep your left hand close to the snap on your dog's collar and make sure there is no slack in the leash.

2   Put a small treat near your eye and say, "Watch me" to get your dog's attention.

3   Tell your dog to stay. If she moves, tighten up on the leash and say, "No," "Sit," and then "Stay" again.

4   Take your right hand and place it in front of your dog's nose. Say "Stay" without bending over. Reward your dog with a small food treat and praise for staying without moving for 5 seconds.

5   Gradually build up this staying time to 10 seconds, then 30 seconds and more before providing a food reward to reinforce this command. Make sure you introduce a release command to get your dog to stop staying. It can be "Okay" or "We're done" or some other easy-to-remember phrase.

TAKE TWO: Once your dog is consistently staying beside you on cue, step up the challenge. You both are ready to introduce different positions, like facing your dog or standing behind him. Be careful in the timing of your treats, however. A common mistake is to reward at the wrong time. If you reach in your pocket for a food treat and your dog gets up, do not give a treat. Otherwise, she will interpret you reaching in your pocket for complying with the "stay" cue. Build on each small success with the goal of getting your dog to stay for longer periods of time and at longer distances from you.

Come Here
MEDIUM ♪♪

GET READY: Treat the "come" cue with respect during training sessions. Resist the temptation to call your dog only to reprimand him for digging in the garden or raiding the kitchen garbage can. By doing so, you unintentionally are training your dog to associate the word "come" with a prelude to punishment—or, at the very least, a signal that playtime and fun is over. Always say "come" in an upbeat tone. Each time your dog heeds your "come" cue, she should be praised so that she equates compliance with positive feedback. Before you start, attach your dog to a long line or leash that is 15 to 20 ft (4–5 m) in length.

1 Begin by holding the end, and let your dog wander around. When she is distracted by something, call her name and command, "Come."

2 If she does not obey, give enough of a tug on the rope to get her attention, then back up, encouraging her to come to you. Once again, the tug on the rope means, "Pay attention to me!" Recognize that your dog may want to avoid the tug on the rope, so she will respond to this training one of two ways. She will either come every time you call her, or she will stop being distracted and will stay close to you even though she is on her long line.

3 Take her for a walk and let her drag the rope. When she becomes distracted, call her name and say, "Come." If she does not come, pick up the rope, and give a tug, making her come. As she heads your way, back up to the spot you were standing when you initially called her. It's time for her to learn that after one command to come, you will enforce it.

4 When your dog comes every time you call on a long rope, you're ready to repeat these steps using a shorter rope or leash no longer than 6 ft (1.8 m).

USING CLICKERS AND TARGET STICKS

To help your dog learn, consider turning to two popular training tools: clickers and target sticks. You use the clicker to associate a behavior to a sound, and a target stick to point to the target. The goal is to condition the dog to repeat an action or pay attention to what the target stick is touching.

🦴 A clicker is a small plastic box with a metal strip inside. When you hold it in your palm and press down on the metal strip, it makes a distinctive click sound. With clicker training, timing is imperative. You click as soon as your dog does an action you desire. And then quickly follow with praise or a small treat. Your dog begins to learn that the click noise tells her that she did what was asked and that a reward is on its way.

🦴 You can also use a target stick to aid in your training sessions. The goal of target training is to teach your dog to touch an object with her paw or nose on cue. Once she learns this basic skill, she can open doors, ring door bells, turn on a wall light switch with her paw and much more.

Tackling Problem Behaviors

Your dog will, at some time or other, exhibit behaviors that are not easy to deal with. That is why learning what to do and when is essential.

Dogs are not born with owner's manuals. They rely on us to teach them what is acceptable and what is not. In movies, on television and comic pages, many of us have been amused by lovable misbehaving dogs. Among them are Marmaduke, Clifford and Scooby Doo. But in the real world, you want and deserve a well-mannered dog. Here are common canine misdeeds with advice on how to react.

Leash Yanking
SCENARIO:

It's not the size of the dog, but the size of her determination to be the boss on walks. Her constant pulling on the leash can knock you off your feet and cause injury to her neck.

SOLUTION:

Bring a small bag of treats on your next outing. Each time your dog stops and heeds your "watch me" cue, dole out a treat. Your goal is to make yourself more important than outside distractions. Secondly, fasten the leash to a harness rather than your dog's collar. Thirdly, when your dog starts to yank, stop moving or abruptly change directions. Give a treat when she complies.

Digging Your Garden
SCENARIO:

You pride yourself on your green-thumb talents to cultivate tasty tomatoes or beautiful begonias. But your dog thrives on being a furry roto-tiller by feverishly pawing, churning up the soil and uprooting your garden goodies.

SOLUTION:

Make your garden less inviting to your dog by creating a "pepper pooch" solution. Mix 2 tablespoons of cayenne pepper and 6 drops of dishwashing soap in a gallon (3.75 l) of water. Place this solution in a spray bottle and apply it to your plants. And compromise by devoting a portion of your backyard to satisfy your dog's gotta-dig tendencies. Buy an inexpensive plastic kiddy pool. Fill it with dirt and hide a few dog treats and toys and then call your dog over to play a fun treasure hunt game.

Crotch-Sniffing Houseguests
SCENARIO:

You greet your visitors with handshakes or hugs. In the canine kingdom, one dog "greets" another by sticking her nose in its back end and sniffing. The canine nose detects details about the other dog, including her age, health condition, what she recently ate and even her mood.

SOLUTION:

Teach your dog to greet two-legged guests in a less embarrassing manner by reinforcing her compliance when told to "sit" and "stay." Then place a small treat in your hand just below your dog's nose and encourage her to paw at the treat. Couple this with "Good shake" so your dog learns that sniffing a houseguest does not yield him the goodies she garners when she sits politely and raises a paw to shake to greet.

Mouthing and Nipping Your Hands and Ankles

SCENARIO:

Puppies use their mouths to explore their environments and to grab your attention. But ouch! Their sharp, tiny teeth can puncture your skin, especially at the delicate (and available) areas of your hands and ankles.

SOLUTION:

Teach your puppy the proper play rules from the start so that she knows she needs to sit on cue before any interactions with people: greeting visitors to the home, engaging in fetch or getting ready to go for a leashed walk. If your puppy's teeth contact your skin, make a high-pitched yelp to let her know it hurt to teach her to inhibit her bite. Don't quickly yank your hand from her mouth because this rapid movement can trigger her play drive. Instead, let your hand go limp as you move it away from her mouth. Finally, offer her a suitable substitute to satisfy her teething needs, like a chew toy.

Train your puppy right from the start not to give love bites. She needs to learn bite inhibition.

Raiding the Kitchen Trash Can
SCENARIO:
As disgusting as it may seem, some dogs find "leftovers" in the kitchen trash can to be deliciously irresistible. But the contents may cause digestive upset and diarrhea in your dog or be toxic, such as chocolate or household cleaning materials.

SOLUTION:
If possible, relocate the trash can inside a pantry or under the kitchen sink and place childproof latches on the door handles. Also, make the trash can less beckoning by spraying dog repellent in it and sprinkling baking soda (a taste most dogs detest). Finally, invest in a trash can with a strong lid.

Leftovers marinating in the kitchen trash seem to beckon some dogs. Beware, as in their quest to seek and eat discarded food, they could get sick from spoiled food.

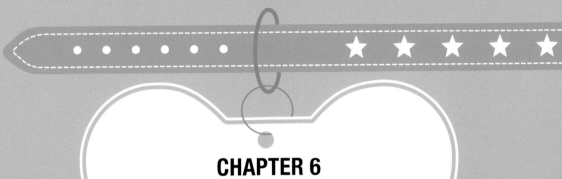

CHAPTER 6
Household Chore Tricks

Household Chore Tricks

Give that adage "working like a dog" a welcome infusion of fun and creativity. Dogs don't want to sit around, taking one nap after the next. Most enjoy getting to do something, especially around the house.

Dogs love to please their favorite people and thrive on praise and this is your chance to put these characteristics to good use. It's time to call on your four-legged friend to assist you in tidying up the house—and even saving a bit on your utility bill.

Fetch the TV Remote
MEDIUM 🐾🐾

GET READY: Make sure your dog is proficient at these cues: fetch, take it and drop it. This is a handy trick so that you don't have to get off the comfy couch if the remote is across the room.

1 Wrap the remote in soft cloth for easy canine gripping. Initially, some dogs do not like the feel of hard plastic in their mouths.

2 Smear a moist treat on the cloth attached to the remote to enhance its appeal. Let your dog smell the remote.

3 Place the remote on a table. Sit next to the table and, in an upbeat tone, point to it and say, "Fetch the remote."

4 When he grabs the remote, say "Bring it" and hold a bigger treat in your hand to encourage him to come your way and drop the remote in your lap.

5 Praise and say, "Good, fetch the remote" so he begins to associate this phrase with getting and dropping the remote.

6 Practice the above steps several times in a 5- to 10-minute training session each time. Ignore his miscues and reward his successes.

TAKE TWO: Remove the cloth wrapping from the remote and repeat. Praise your dog for softly mouthing the remote and quickly dole out treats when he complies.

WARNING!

If your dog is still young and in the must-chew-everything stage, delay on teaching this trick until he is older and less destructive. You don't want your dog to accidentally bite down hard on the remote and on the batteries inside the casing. Exposure to the battery acid can cause serious chemical burns in his mouth and throat. So, play it safe! Once he fetches the remote, you can expand this trick to have your dog bring you other items, such as your slippers or socks.

Dogs who love daily walks to new places can be taught to master the art of fetching their own leashes.

Grab Your Leash
MEDIUM 🦴🦴

GET READY: Teach this trick to a dog who enjoys taking leashed walks and has mastered the "fetch" cue.

1 Keep your dog's leash in one location, perhaps near the front or back door.

2 Say to your dog, "Want to go for a walk?" Then point to the leash and say "Leash" as you playfully engage in a mini tug-of-war with the leash in his mouth.

3 Say "Drop it" and attach the leash to his collar or harness. This helps him associate that verbal word with his leash.

4 When the time arrives for your regular daily walk, look at the leash, point at it and say in an upbeat tone, "Want to go for a walk? Grab your leash!"

5 When he heads to the leash and gets it in his mouth, repeat, "Grab your leash" and treat him immediately when he brings it to you.

6 Immediately tether the leash to his collar or harness after he performs this trick so that you provide him an added reward: a walk for complying.

 TAKE TWO: Once your dog realizes that bringing you his leash will result in going on a walk, he may start dropping the leash in your lap. Take him for a quick walk or distract him by having him perform a different trick indoors that reaps a reward and stash the leash out of sight.

Ring a Bell
MEDIUM 🦴🦴

GET READY: This trick, when properly taught and reinforced, makes it crystal clear that ringing the bell is your dog's notice that he needs to potty. You need to be willing to quickly heed your dog's bell ringing in the beginning in order to achieve this trick. Be consistent in taking him outside, praising when he urinates or defecates outside and bringing him back. Treat him only when he completes his bathroom duties. If your dog is ringing the bell more often than usual, he may have a urinary infection. If so, consult your veterinarian.

1 Select a bell on an elastic tether or leash. Show it to your dog and ring the bell.

2 Encourage your dog to sniff and paw at the bell and reward these behaviors with praise and treats.

3 Teach your dog that the name for this object is "bell."

4 Hang the bell on the door you use to take your dog out for a walk—or access to your fenced-in backyard.

5 Hold a treat behind the bell and urge your dog to come over. Encourage him to paw the bell. When his pawing makes the bell ring, say "Ring the bell" and treat.

6 Quickly leash him up and take him outside. Praise him when he potties and bring him back inside. Timing is crucial because you want your dog to adopt a new habit and association that whenever he needs to use the bathroom, he needs to alert you by ringing the bell.

Flip On/Off the Lights
HARD 🦴🦴🦴

GET READY: Your dog will need to have learned the "sit," "touch it," "leap up" and "watch me" cues before attempting this trick. This trick applies only for the wall light switches with toggles or flips to turn on and off. This training is best suited for medium to large dogs. For a small dog, you can train him to jump up on a solid box placed against the wall and just under the light switch.

1 Stand next to a light switch that is easy for your dog to reach. Ask him to sit.

2 Hold a treat on the wall just an inch above the light switch. Tap it a few times against the wall as you encourage your dog to leap up with his front paws near the treat. Give him the treat and praise.

3 Repeat the above step a few times so your dog gets used to leaping up and touching the wall with his front paws.

4 Tap the light switch with one hand as you hold the treat in your closed hand just above the light switch. Say, "Get the lights!" when his paw touches the light switch. Praise and treat.

5 Once your dog is consistently pawing the light switch, put your hand down at your side that contains the treat. Tap the light switch, say "Get the lights!" and reward only when your dog paws the light switch and then sits down.

6 Gradually move farther from the light switch and motion your dog toward it and say "Get the lights!"

Tidy Up Your Toys
HARD ♪♪♪

GET READY: Keep all but a few of your dog's toys in a big, open container. Rotate some toys every few days to maintain your dog's interest in them. Your dog is ready to learn this advanced trick if he consistently heeds the "fetch" and "drop it" cues. He should also know a few of his favorite toys by one-word names so that he can correctly pick up the specific toys to help you tidy up.

1 Place a few plush toys on the floor and call your dog over.

2 Point at the first toy and say, "Fetch" and "Bring it."

3 Position yourself next to your dog's toy box with its lid off.

4 When your dog approaches the toy box with a toy in his mouth, place a treat a few inches above the toy box's opening. This will cause him to drop the toy in the box in order to be able to eat the treat. Say "Good, tidy up!" and treat again and praise.

5 Point to the next toy, call it by its name and repeat the above steps.

6 Point to the final toy and repeat the above steps.

TAKE TWO: Once your dog is consistent in dropping the toy in the box in order to garner the treat inside the box, call out the "tidy up" cue, point to the scattered toys on the floor and point to the toy box. This time, tell him to "Drop it" and then give him a treat. Repeat so he learns that he earns his tasty reward after he completes his housekeeping duties.

🐾 **When there is clutter in your home, you can always benefit by having an extra set of hands (make that four paws) to tidy up.**

Bring Me a Tissue
HARD 🦴🦴🦴

GET READY: Your dog must be able to ace the "fetch," "drop it," "give" and "take it" cues. He must also know how to hold an object gently in a soft mouth so that he does not tear the tissue on his way to you. Expect some boxes of tissues to be "sacrificed" during the tutoring, so buy inexpensive brands.

1. Add double-sided duct tape to the bottom of a tissue box and stick to the floor to keep it from moving. Fluff up the top tissue.

2. Move the tissue and tell your dog to "Take it." Treat and praise when he grabs the top tissue.

3. Tell him, "Give" and treat and praise when he brings you the tissue.

4. Sit down facing the taped tissue box and point to it and then say, "Achoo! Fetch!" Treat and praise when he goes over to grab the top tissue. Remind him to return with it by saying "Give."

5. Now move the tissue box to a table and tape the bottom (be sure that the tape does not mark your tabletop finish).

6. Repeat the first four steps so your dog is comfortable getting the tissue from the table.

 TAKE TWO: Add a fun finish to this trick by pretending to blow your nose into the fetched tissue. Wad it up and give it back to your dog. With a treat inside your hand, lure your dog over to an open and empty wastebasket. Point to the wastebasket and drop the treat into the wastebasket. Say "Drop it" as your dog lets go of the tissue in the wastebasket in order to access the treat. Praise. Keep moving the wastebasket farther away to improve your dog's duration and distance skills.

CHAPTER 7

Basic
Show Tricks

Basic Show Tricks

Trick training boosts communication between you and your canine as well as reinforcing basic obedience commands of "Sit," "Stay," "Come" and "Down." It provides both mental and physical stimulation for your dog.

When you train your canine student to wave or roll over, it is more than just a fun trick to entertain friends and family. Some dogs respond well to the toss of a Frisbee or ball. What "currency" motivates your dog the most? Whatever you use, remember that the behavior should result in your dog earning the treat/reward. Rewards can be treats or praise with lots of petting, although the treat should not produce the behavior.

Practice performance tricks for 5 minutes, a few times a day, and one trick at a time until your dog has mastered it. Always end the training session on a positive note. If your dog aces shaking paws two times in a row after messing up a couple times, heap on the praise. Say "Class is over" and then treat her to a therapeutic massage or a walk. Pick a favorite activity for your dog to reinforce that you are pleased with how she did in "canine school."

Shake Hands
EASY
GET READY: Your dog needs to have mastered the "Sit" cue to be able to lift her paw to shake hands for this trick. Meanwhile, you need small treats ready to hand out.

1 Face your dog and say "Shake," gently lift your dog's front right paw into the air with your left hand.

2 Once her paw is raised, say, "Good" immediately and reward with a treat.

3 Release your dog's paw and let it touch the ground.

4 Wait a few seconds and then, holding the treat in your right hand, repeat steps 2 and 3 until your dog recognizes that the word "Shake" means a treat if she raises her front paw.

5 After a few assists from you, say the word, "Shake" without lifting your dog's paw. Hold the treat in front of her to motivate her to lift her paw on her own. Immediately praise and treat when she does.

 TAKE TWO: Another way to train your dog to shake hands is to start out by tickling the back of her front legs, just above her paws with your left hand. Have your right hand ready to reach for her paw as she lifts it because of the tickling. When this happens, quickly say, "Shake" and grasp her lifted paw gently. Say "Good" and promptly release her paw and hand over a treat.

Once your dog has mastered shaking with her right paw, train her to shake with her left front paw and do a double shake of right paw-left paw.

Do the Canine Wave
MEDIUM 🦴🦴

GET READY: This is the ideal trick to teach your dog once she has mastered the "shake" and is a terrific and polite action for your dog to greet people rather than leaping up on them. Your dog should be in the "sit" position and you should have treats on hand.

1 Face your dog and say, "Shake." When your dog's right front paw reaches out to you, move your left hand slightly, so that you don't make contact.

2 When your dog starts pawing at the air, label this action by saying "Wave."

3 Reward each time your dog raises her paw in the air even for a few seconds when you say "Wave" and follow that with "Good," then give her a treat.

4 Repeat until your dog understands that "Wave" means to move her raised paw back and forth. Your goal is to be able to eventually skip the "Shake" cue and only give the "Wave" cue to have your dog respond.

TAKE TWO: Once your dog is waving consistently on cue, you can start to work on improving her wave motions. Don't reward for every wave she delivers, but only the better ones to make her want to work harder and earn a treat.

🐾 Dogs of any size or age can quickly learn to greet by shaking paws. Invest a few minutes each day to help achieve this hello.

Speak
EASY ♪

GET READY: Identify what triggers your dog to bark—most likely the ringing of your doorbell. You need to have a friend willing to ring or knock on your front door to encourage your dog to bark. Your goal is to reward your dog when she speaks on cue with a few alert barks and also to reward her when she finds the canine "mute" button and stops barking on cue.

1 Have your friend stand outside the front door with you inside with your dog on the leash facing the door.

2 When your friend rings the doorbell, quickly say "Speak" just before your dog starts to bark. Your goal is to have your dog associate "Speak" with her cue to bark.

3 Repeat this a few times and only reward when your dog barks every time you ask her to "Speak."

4 Skip having the door bell rung and ask your dog to "Speak" and reward when she barks.

 TAKE TWO: Now you are ready to introduce the "Hush" part. Mimic the actions of a traffic cop by holding your open palm in front of your non-barking dog. Say "Hush" and give her a treat. Practice the "hush" a few times and then ask your dog to "speak." Only give her a treat when she barks for the "speak" request.

Roll Over
MEDIUM ♪♪
GET READY: Your dog must know how to perform "Down" when asked and must feel at ease on her back. Condition her to feel secure on her back by treating her to playful belly rubs.

1 Get your dog to be in a down position facing you and kneel in front of her.

2 Strategically place a treat in your closed hand and place your hand on the right side of her head.

3 Steadily move the treat from the side of her head back toward her right shoulder blade while saying, "Roll over." She should roll over on her side. Then say "Good" and hand over the treat.

4 Once she is consistently rolling on her side, continue moving your hand holding the treat over her shoulder blades and her backbone. She will be moving her head and then her body to get to the treat. She may need your assistance to completely flip over.

5 Once she flips over, quickly mark that action by saying "Roll over" and treat.

6 When she is rolling over on verbal cues, pair this with a hand signal of your outstretched hand doing a circle in the air.

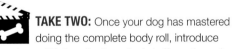 **TAKE TWO:** Once your dog has mastered doing the complete body roll, introduce the phrase "Belly up" when she is halfway through the roll with her belly exposed and her back on the ground. With treats and timing, she will soon learn to stop on her back with her paws up in the air when you say, "Belly up."

Your dog must heed the "watch me" cue in order to be successful at performing doggy push-ups.

Doggy Pushups
MEDIUM ♪♪

GET READY: Your dog must already know how to go into a "sit" and a "down" when you say those words or use specific hand signals for those actions. This is a fun trick that gives your dog a quick workout.

1 Face your dog and ask her to "Sit."

2 Hold a treat in front of her nose.

3 Say "Down" as you quickly move the treat straight down to the floor in front of your dog's paws. Give a treat.

4 Then take another treat and say "Sit" enthusiastically as you hoist the treat straight up to get your dog out of the down position and into the sit position.

5 Once your dog heeds the "Sit" and the "Down," you are ready to put them together in one sit-down cue. Only give a treat and praise when your dog completes the sit-down combination.

Getting your dog to quickly sit and plop down and spring back up a few times is a fun way to show off her many talents to others. It is also a great aerobic workout.

Take A Bow
MEDIUM 𝄪

GET READY: The play bow pose (with the dog's rear up in the air and her front legs outstretched and lowered) is the universal "let's play" and "I'm friendly" signal in the canine world. For this trick to work, be upbeat and enthusiastic in this training session to inspire your dog to up her playfulness.

1 Start with your dog in a stance facing you.

2 Get her to lower her head by holding a treat in your closed hand at her nose height.

3 Gently touch her nose with this hand for her to smell the treat and lower your hand down while saying, "Take a bow."

4 When her front elbows touch the floor, say, "Take a bow" and immediately hand over the treat. Praise her for a job well done.

5 Repeat these steps about 10 times each day in your mini training sessions and only dole out the treat when she lowers the front of her body while raising her back end.

Drop It
MEDIUM 🎵🎵

GET READY: For this trick, you will need two treats—one regarded as Grade-A by your dog and one that merits just a so-so response from your dog. Or, if your dog is highly toy motivated, bring her favorite toy and one she is a bit blasé about into this training lesson. This is a trust-building trick. You are teaching her that by giving up a resource, she stands a good chance of receiving one of greater value.

1 Play with your dog's face and mouth and give a treat as long as she does not nip.

2 Gently place one hand over her muzzle and the other hand under her chin to open her mouth. Speak in a happy tone, close her mouth, and then give her a treat. You want her to get used to having her mouth opened by you.

3 Show her the so-so level toy and get her to grab it in her mouth. Do this by playing a quick game of fetch or tug-of-war.

4 With the toy in her mouth, say "Drop it" and hold up the Grade-A level toy.

5 As soon as she drops the so-so toy, say, "Good, drop it" and hand over the Grade-A level toy to her.

6 With the Grade-A level toy in her mouth, hold up her favorite treat and say "Drop it." When she drops the toy, hand over the treat and praise her.

 TAKE TWO: If your dog won't release the so-so toy in step 4, try tugging on the side of her rib cage to cause her to open her mouth. Once she has this trick down, teach her to approach you with the toy in her mouth and give it to you when you say, "Give."

Sit Pretty
MEDIUM 🐾🐾
GET READY: Your dog must be able to get into a sit position quickly and on cue. She should not have any health issues that would make it unsafe for her to balance her weight on her back legs.

1 Face your small dog and have her in a sit.

2 Kneel close to her with a treat in your closed palm.

3 Hold the treat at her nose and slowly lift your hand up and say "Sit pretty."

4 To prevent her from jumping up and lifting her hind legs off the floor, stay close and lower the treat further in front of her nose.

5 When she balances on her hind legs, say, "Good, sit pretty!" and immediately treat. Strive to have her sit up a few seconds longer once she is sitting up consistently.

TAKE TWO: For medium and large dogs, the technique is different. Put your dog in a sit and then stand behind her with her rear end and hind legs between your two feet. Take a treat in your closed hand and direct it at her nose and then lift your hand slowly up. Let her brace her back against your body while she learns to balance on her hind feet. You may need to brace her chest with your non-treat hand against your legs to improve her balance.

TRAINING ENVIRONMENT
When introducing a new trick to your dog, make sure your "class room" is in a quiet, distraction-free location within your home. Build on that success in this controlled environment by:

🦴 Increasing the distance between you and your dog as tricks are achieved.

🦴 Pairing a hand signal with the verbal cue for the specific trick. This way, your dog can heed your requests by sight or by sound.

🦴 Speeding up your dog's execution of the trick by rewarding only for quickest times.

🦴 Extending the duration of time for your dog to perform a trick. For example, she may need to wave back and forth three times before earning a treat.

🦴 Moving into the backyard or dog-safe outdoor places where there are distractions to see if she can focus her attention on you.

CHAPTER 8

Advanced Show Tricks

Advanced Show Tricks

Think of your four-legged friend as a forever student of life who loves to learn. Your dog can't wait to try a new trick and then garner your attention and affection when she aces it.

Think of training as building on past successes. This section contains advanced crowd-pleasing tricks that evolved from the canine basic obedience hallmarks. With your dog as your ready partner, here are tips and tactics to teach your dog tricks that merit an impressive response from family and friends.

Fetch a Toy by Name
MEDIUM 🎵🎵

GET READY: Every time you play with your dog with one of his toys, give that toy a distinctive, short, one-word name. Say that name every time you play together because dogs learn by repetition. For this trick, your dog must be consistent at fetching and have a pure joy for various canine toys. He also needs to be focused and really listen to you and not be so overly excited that he simply dashes over to pick up any toy in this trick.

1 In a quiet room free of distractions, line up one of your dog's favorite toys (perhaps a tennis ball) on the ground with two small household items, such as a screwdriver and a hairbrush.

2 Call your dog over. Let him inspect each object, but do not let him pick up his toy.

3 Touch his toy and energetically say, "Find your ball." Praise and treat as soon as he goes over and touches the ball. Heap on more treats when he picks up the ball and brings it back to you.

4 Repeat this a few times to make sure your dog starts to associate "Ball" with fetching the tennis ball.

5 Replace the hairbrush with one of your dog's other favorite toys, such as a rope tug.

6 Touch the rope tug toy and say, "Rope" to encourage him to fetch it. Praise when he correctly brings the rope toy to you.

7 If he brings the wrong object, don't say anything and don't treat or praise. Simply get him back into a sit position and line up the three objects and start again.

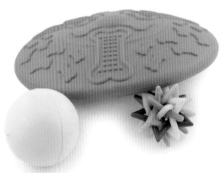

Spin in Circles
EASY 🦴

GET READY: Your dog needs to heed the "Watch me" cue and be able to easily follow hand movements.

1 Put your dog in a standing position facing you.

2 With a treat in your closed right hand, let him sniff it.

3 Move your closed hand in a circular clockwise direction and say "Spin" so as he is led by his nose to pursue the treat.

4 Give the treat when your dog completes a full circle and say "Spin, good!"

5 Once your dog is moving in a circle, switch and have him circle around you in a counterclockwise direction.

TAKE TWO: Add a hand signal to this trick by taking your non-treat hand and moving it in a circle while saying "Spin." Move it first clockwise and then test your dog's level of smartness to see if he will switch and move counterclockwise when you move your hand in a counterclockwise direction.

 This trick works best if you are long-legged or you have a short-legged dog.

Weave Between Your Legs
MEDIUM ♪♪

GET READY: You need to strike a balance between having your dog being attentive but not too energetic, because you need to work on your timing and balance. He needs to know the "watch me" cue and happily follow hand signals. This is a key trick used in the popular sport of agility with the canine weaving in and out of stationary poles.

1 Stand with your legs apart and put your dog in a sit directly behind you.

2 With a treat in your closed hand, reach through your legs and call your dog to come.

3 When he pokes his head through your legs, say, "Good peek" and give a treat.

4 Practice having him poke his head through your legs and looking up at you for a few days. Make it playful and fun.

5 Now position your dog in a stance on your right side and take a big step forward with your left leg.

6 With treats in your left hand, lower this hand under your left outstretched leg to get your dog to put his head under your legs.

7 Lure him to move under your legs and move your hand with the treats forward in front of you. As soon as your dog completes moving under your legs, say, "Weave, good!" and treat.

8 Gradually expand the hand-luring motion and treat only when your dog successfully weaves through your legs.

TAKE TWO: Strive to have your dog perform a figure-8 weave in, under and around your legs by luring him with the treat in your lead hand. The hand signal for weaving is an open palm placed under your outstretched thigh of your leg that is forward.

Crawl
MEDIUM 🐾🐾
GET READY: Your dog needs to comply with the "watch me" and "come" cues and have the physical ability to move with his body lowered.

1 Face your dog and have him in a down stance.

2 Kneel down and place a closed hand containing treats on the floor directly in front of his nose.

3 To help convey his need to crawl and not stand up, say the word, "c-r-a-w-l" in a drawn-out manner as you slowly move the hand with the treats about 1 ft (30 cm) from his nose.

4 If he tries to stand up, gently keep your other hand on his shoulders and slow down the pace of moving the hand with the treat away from his nose.

5 Once he does crawl to get the treat, immediately say, "Good, crawl!" and hand over the treats. Praise him.

6 Gradually stand up and lift one of your feet with the heel still on the ground and place a few treats under there. Tell your dog to crawl over to fetch these treats. If he stands up, lightly step on the treats.

 TAKE TWO: When you catch your dog crawling on his own, mark it with "Good, crawl" and praise him. You can jazz up this trick by holding a long pole about 2 ft (60 cm) above ground in front of your dog, who is in a down position. Say, "Crawl" and lure the treat under the pole to get him to follow it by scooting forward. Say "Good, crawl" as you slowly move the treat to guide him under and forward past the pole. Praise and treat.

Back Up
HARD 🦴🦴🦴

GET READY: Your dog must be able to come quickly when called, watch you for guidance, and be confident moving backward. Choose a hallway or narrow path to minimize your dog's potential to move side to side instead of back.

1 Face your dog, who is standing, and hold a treat in your closed hand right in front of him nose. Allow him to sniff.

2 Gently press your hand with the treat against his nose and say "Back up."

3 As you press on his nose, slowly walk toward your dog to force her to go backward.

4 Lift your knee and gently press it against his chest. When your dog moves a few steps back, say, "Good, back up" and treat.

5 If your dog sits instead of backs up, adjust and make sure that your hand holding the treat is at his nose height and not below that.

TAKE TWO: Slowly stop pressing your hand against his nose and your knee against his chest. Introduce a "back up" hand signal that consists of moving your non-treat open hand from your chest forward toward your dog and say, "Back up."

🐾 **Lightweight small dogs with a sense of balance fare best in mastering the Back Up trick.**

Play Dead
MEDIUM 🐾🐾
GET READY: This trick is harder than it seems and definitely worthy of applause. Your dog must consistently heed the "stay" and "roll over" cues before learning this advanced trick.

1 Put your dog in a down and face him.

2 With treats in one hand, lure him to his right side but steady his body when he is belly up and has not completely rolled over.

3 Softly say, "Stay" to encourage him to remain belly up and motionless. Lightly place your non-treat hand on his belly to hold this position.

4 Introduce the "Bang, you're dead" verbal and hand signals. The hand signal should be making your non-treat hand look like it is a handgun with your thumb up, your index finger out, and your other three fingers pressed against your palm.

5 Say, "Bang, you're dead" and use the hand signal when your dog is in belly up, then treat. You want to reinforce that rewards come when he is belly up and quiet.

6 Come up with a fun release cue, such as "You're alive" or "You're bulletproof," spoken in an energetic tone to have him flip over, stand and come to you.

The best time to teach the Play Dead trick is when your dog is tired after a long run or game of fetch and is relaxed. The key to success is making this a calm, quiet maneuver.

CHAPTER 9

Socializing

Meeting and Greeting

Dogs are social beings. Hopefully, during your canine's lifetime she will get to form strong friendships with people of all ages as well as a pack of dogs and even cats. Learn the art of introducing your dog to many.

Do you instantly like everyone you meet? Are there some people who grate on your nerves or who you don't wish to interact with again? Your dog is no different. Just like us, dogs have favorites among people and other pets, and they definitely display their disdain for others. Set your dog up for success by socializing her properly and teaching her how to play with a purpose. The sooner you can introduce fun and positive learning to your puppy or newly adopted dog, the less likely you'll have to deal with serious behavior problems with her.

Socializing Your Puppy

You need to find effective ways to get your puppy acclimatized to the outside world. Once her set of puppy vaccines to bolster her immune system is done, consider these outings:

THE SUPERMARKET

Spend 15 minutes once a week in front of your supermarket with your puppy. This busy place will allow your puppy to meet all types of people, including hat-wearers, little children, and individuals in wheelchairs.

OUTDOOR CAFÉ

Bring your puppy with you to an outdoor café. Be sure to bring a portable bowl, a bottle of water, and a few tasty treats for your puppy.

ERRANDS

Take your puppy with you on quick errands to pick up dry cleaning, or order a quick lunch from a fast-food restaurant drive-thru.

DOG PARTIES

Host weekly backyard dog parties with a few of your friends and their well-behaved canines. Select an enclosed yard where you can supervise play. Your puppy gets the chance to learn from adult dogs through play.

NEIGHBORHOOD DOG WALKS

Organize neighborhood dog walks and have these dogs join you in a 30-minute jaunt weekly to introduce your puppy to a variety of dogs.

Pet-to-Pet Introductions

This union of dog-to-dog, cat-to-dog and cat-to-cat won't magically occur overnight. But set your pets up for success each step of the way and you will achieve a furry Brady Bunch.

It's natural to want to quickly present your resident dog with the newest addition to your family. After all, we're only human. But in your excitement, don't rush them and certainly don't put them face to face immediately. Patience must be practiced. No matter if your resident dog is now sharing life under your roof with another dog, cat, bird or other pet, set everyone up for success—and possibly, the start of lifetime friendships by following this step-by-step introduction plan:

PREPARE THE GREETING ROOM.

Before bringing home the new pet, set up a "safe" room in your house ahead of time that contains pet necessities for your newcomer. That includes toys, food and water bowls, pet bed, and perhaps a radio set on a talk show to get her used to conversations that occur in your home.

WELCOME THE SNIFF GAME.

The best way to introduce your resident dog to any newcomer is not by sight, but by scent. Don't interfere or say anything when your resident dog tracks down the scent of a newcomer by sniffing under the closed door.

SPLIT YOUR PET TIME.

Devote time to each pet separately for a few days as everyone adjusts to the change in the household.

PERFORM THE TOWEL INTRODUCTION TEST.

Take a hand towel and rub it over the face and back of your resident dog. Then head into the new pet's room and do the same. And, do another round so that the towel technique successfully exchanges scents between the two of them. This is important because it is best for pets to get to know each other initially by smell. And, the toweling makes each smell a bit like the other one.

PERMIT PEEKING AT MEALTIME.

Use a see-through pet door gate or other barrier at dinner time. Allow the resident dog and newcomer to meet with this safe buffer between them while they dine.

Dog to Dog

Like us, dogs are socially minded, but they also have their favorites and foes when it comes to other dogs and cats. Introductions are key and that's where you intervene.

When introducing your dog to another dog (who may or may not join your household), choose a neutral turf so that your dog won't view this newcomer as a territorial intruder. Both dogs should be on leashes. You hold your dog's leash and someone else maintains control of the other dog. Let the two dogs sniff each other, a normal canine greeting, and speak in a friendly, positive tone. After 10 seconds or so, separate the dogs and give each of them treats for obeying a "sit" or "stay" command. Then, walk the dogs, keeping them apart. Occasionally stop to allow them to sniff one another and provide more treats when this is successful.

Your goal here is to create a good mood to encourage these dogs to be friendly. Watch their body postures. Things are going well if they go into what's called a "play bow" (front legs on the ground, head lowered, and back end raised high in the air). If either dog is emitting deep growls or an icy stare, disrupt them by calmly and positively calling them, having them sit and giving them a treat to avoid these gestures escalating into acts of aggression.

Once the dogs appear to be pals, bring them home for the second round of introductions. Initially, give preference for treats and toys to the resident dog but realize that, in time, dogs will establish their own social ranking.

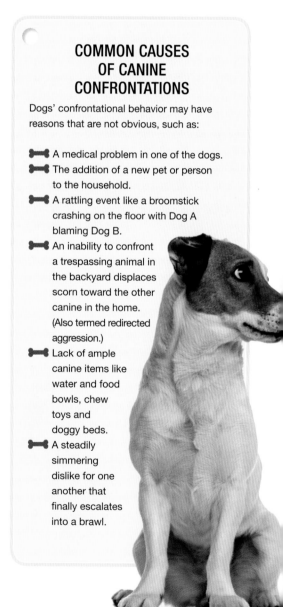

COMMON CAUSES OF CANINE CONFRONTATIONS

Dogs' confrontational behavior may have reasons that are not obvious, such as:

- A medical problem in one of the dogs.
- The addition of a new pet or person to the household.
- A rattling event like a broomstick crashing on the floor with Dog A blaming Dog B.
- An inability to confront a trespassing animal in the backyard displaces scorn toward the other canine in the home. (Also termed redirected aggression.)
- Lack of ample canine items like water and food bowls, chew toys and doggy beds.
- A steadily simmering dislike for one another that finally escalates into a brawl.

When introducing your dog to a new canine, pay attention to their body language and know when to intervene before any growls occur.

How to Safely Stop a Dog Fight

If your dog tangles with another dog, keep yourself safe by breaking up the fight using the following approaches:

- Throwing a sweatshirt or jacket on the dogs to distract them.
- Lodging a backpack, board or any big object in between the two dogs.
- Spraying the dogs with water if a garden hose is near.
- Pulling the back legs of the dog starting the fight. Use your elbow on her shoulders to pin her. Ideally, if someone else is present, use this "wheelbarrow" maneuver on both dogs at the same time. You need to lift the back legs off the ground.
- Keeping your fingers together (harder for a dog to bite than fingers apart) and grabbing the back fur or tail of the attacking dog. Keep away from the dog's head.

After the fight, do a complete head-to-tail inspection of your dog and be sure to examine inside her mouth for any injuries. Take your dog to your veterinarian if you see any bites, even minor ones. Dog bites can be easily disguised by fur, can involve deep layers of skin and muscle, and can easily become infected.

Dog to Cat

When introducing a cat to your dog, you do need to think like a cat and a dog. Your goal is to set both up for success with the hope of a lifelong friendship together.

The truth about cats and dogs is that many form close friendships. Use that canine hierarchical mindset to your advantage. Dogs want to know clearly where they rank in the family. They don't care if they are last, even behind the pet mouse. What they don't tolerate is canine confusion caused by one family member treating them like a king—and ranking above the family cat—while another family member designates the dog at a ranking below the cat. To keep hair from flying and hissy fits from occurring, you need to demonstrate to your dog in action and attitude that the family cat outranks her and for her to respect the cat. Here is some key advice to achieve this goal of dog to cat respect:

🐾 Feed felines first and have your dog sit in the "park" position to wait for their bowls.

🐾 Keep your dog in a down, stay position at the back patio door so that your harnessed cat can saunter out to your fenced backyard for supervised outings. Don't let your dog re-enter the home until you say, "Ok, let's go!"

🐾 Greet your cat first and then your dog when you come home.

How to Settle In

When you bring your new puppy or dog to a home with a resident cat, there are certain strategies to follow:

🐾 Recognize that dogs and cats act differently. When first introducing your new dog to your resident cat, keep the dog on a leash or inside a crated kennel. Let your cat go up and investigate the dog on her terms. If she flees the room, let her go. Don't chase her because that can trigger the prey drive in your new dog. If necessary, step on your dog's leash to keep her from chasing the cat.

☙ Offer your best food treats to your new dog whenever your resident cat enters the room. This consistent action will instill in your canine that whenever the cat is around, good things happen, like tasty treats. She will begin to look forward to seeing the cat.

☙ Allow for escape routes for your resident cat from your new dog by keeping the bedroom door open (so your cat can scoot under the bed) or by providing safe, high perches out of your dog's reach. Teach your dog that some places in the household are for cats only. It is a lesson she will heed for the rest of her life.

☙ Recognize the difference between a playful romp and a deadly pursuit by your dog toward your cat. A happy dog will get into a play bow with front paws extended out and head tucked into her chin at the start of a friendly game of chase. A play-seeking cat will display a relaxed posture and not hiss or growl. Stop the chase as soon as you hear a low growl or hiss. Your dog will learn to play on your cat's terms.

DISTRACTION TACTICS

Teaching the "Watch me" command can effectively distract a dog from doing something aggressive toward your new cat. You can teach this with or without a clicker (the clicker may make learning a bit easier if your dog is clicker-trained).

Start by getting your dog's attention with a morsel of something yummy. Hold the food in your fingers and get your dog's attention with it. Bring it up to your face so that your pet is looking into your eyes. Say, "Watch me! Good!" and give your dog the food once she makes eye contact. Do this several times. Each time your dog makes eye contact after the "Watch me!" command, you give praise and treats. Slowly lengthen the amount of time between the command and the treat.

Dogs and Humans

Family members range from infants to great-grandparents and everyone in between. Because of this, it is crucial that you positively expose your dog to a variety of people when she is a puppy or quickly after you adopt.

During the lifetime of your dog, your household situation may change. You may get a new boyfriend or girlfriend, marry or divorce, have a baby, or welcome your aging parents or grandparents to live with you. Your dog needs to know how to fit in with all these generations under one roof.

Kids

Whether you are a new mom or preparing your home for houseguests who are bringing a baby or toddler, you can take steps to protect the baby and minimize stress in your dog:

🐾 Supervise whenever your dog is in the same room with an infant or small child to protect both of them. A sudden movement or grab by an infant can cause a dog to react by growling or snapping. Speak calmly and confidently to your dog around infants and young children to help your dog feel at ease at all times.

🐾 Teach your young children the right way to touch and approach a puppy or dog. Practice first with a stuffed animal and show your child how to pet slowly and softly and to never pull on the ears or tails or hit, kick or throw objects at pets.

🐾 Remind children to never disturb a dog when she is sleeping or eating. A startled or threatened dog may react to these situations by growling, barking, nipping or even biting to protect her self and her resources.

🐾 Praise and encourage children when they do something nice for your dog or help with canine chores such as filling the water bowl. Praise reinforces the development of pet responsibility skills and helps to strengthen the friendship and trust between children and the family dog.

Spouse or Houseguests

Some dogs need time to feel comfortable around houseguests, or permanent additions to your household, such as a new spouse or roommate. Encourage the new adults to practice patience when getting to know the resident dog. Instruct them to have the dog get in a sit position before greeting them. Advise them to not engage in rough playing with the dog, such as wrestling or tug-of-war, because it can escalate from play into fights. Another beneficial idea is to invite trusted neighbors and friends to stop by and play with your dog to improve her socialization skills. Give them treats to dole out when your dog performs a good behavior, like sitting or coming when called. Your dog will look forward to these visits.

🐶 If your dog is hesitant at first in meeting someone, never force the introduction. Let your dog stay in the room and have time to feel comfortable with this new person.

Dogs to Birds and/or Mice

Even though your dog can count on you providing her with nutritious meals, she still may be tempted to unleash her instinctive predatory nature toward the family bird or mouse, so try to discourage such behavior where possible.

Even if your dog seems blasé around small creatures, never leave them unsupervised. Always make sure that the bird or mouse is tucked safely in its cage out of access from your dog. Separate them if your dog displays these predatory signs:

- Stares fixedly at the bird or mouse.
- Folds her ears back and closes her mouth.
- Leans forward, putting more weight on her front paws.

That said, some dogs do tone down their predatory natures and become buddies with birds and mice. So if you desire to have a home filled with wings and fur, take extra precautions to keep birds and mice safe at all times.

THERAPY DOGS

Never under-estimate the power of the tail wag. Well-socialized therapy dogs are visiting in greater numbers at senior care centers, hospitals and schools. They provide residents, patients, students and staff with many health benefits. Among my favorite pluses that therapy dogs offer:

🦴 Therapy dogs aid in improving fine motor skills in nursing home residents, who may be more motivated to open a jar to retrieve a treat to feed the visiting dog or use her hand to pet the dog from the top of the head to the base of the tail.

🦴 Therapy dogs encourage children with special needs, like autism or behavior disorders, to improve their communication skills by "speaking" with these trained dogs.

🦴 Therapy dogs elevate moods for people coping with anxiety issues or depression.

🦴 Therapy dogs provide unconditional, uncomplicated friendship. During their visits, they don't have any hidden agendas or demands. And, they don't judge those they visit.

The best therapy dogs are friendly, outgoing and confident. It is as if they have never met a stranger or been in a strange place. Here are some qualifications required to become a registered therapy dog:

🦴 Is healthy and current on vaccinations, including rabies
🦴 Is clean and well groomed
🦴 Enjoys meeting and interacting with people
🦴 Likes to travel
🦴 Accepts being petted and touched
🦴 Tolerates noises and medical equipment
🦴 Adapts to new surroundings easily
🦴 Heeds cues to "leave it" to avoid anything spilled on a floor, like medication.

Party Games

One of the best ways to sneak in good doggy manners in a fun way is to host a dog party. A few years ago, I boldly created a new national holiday in the United States: National Dog Party Day.

Just like us, dogs learn best when the atmosphere is fun and full of positive, can-do energy. At my parties, all dogs are on leashes and bring their "dates"—their favorite person. Dogs get the chance to participate in a variety of games and gobble up healthy treats. At the heart of special dog parties are games.

More and more people are celebrating their dogs' birthdays with parties that include games and bone-shaped birthday cakes.

Snoopy Says
EASY 🦴

HOW TO PLAY: This is a variation of the popular children's game called Simon Says. Instruct guests to line up with their leashed dogs. The people-dog teams must comply with our commands whenever we say, "Snoopy says." For example, "Snoopy says sit your dog." People must get their dogs to sit within 5 seconds or less. But if we simply say, "Sit your dog," people who do so are eliminated from the competition. The winning team is the one that heeds all "Snoopy says" commands.

🐾 **Dogs are the original party animals and need and deserve to celebrate special events in a fun setting.**

Wacky Walks
EASY 🦴

HOW TO PLAY: Bring a pocketful of small treats with you. As you are walking with her by your side, practice basic obedience commands like "Sit" and reward your dog when she complies. Then teach her to go different speeds by saying "Slow" and getting your dog to take very slow steps. Then speed up the pace by saying, "Fast, fast, fast" and reward your dog for moving quickly. Also vary the time and location of your walks so you give your dog the chance to sniff and inspect new places. These tactics make the walk become a fun learning session and reinforces your dog to pay close attention to you because she never knows when a tasty treat will be doled out.

Canine Musical Chairs
MEDIUM 🦴🦴

HOW TO PLAY: Line up hula hoops on the ground, spaced about 3 ft (1 m) apart on the ground. Intentionally start with one less hula hoop than the number of participants. Instruct the participants to leash their dogs and to walk single file in a counterclockwise fashion around the hula hoops. Play dog-themed music as the participants walk their leashed dogs around the hula hoops. When the music abruptly stops, each guest must get their dog to sit inside a hula hoop and each person must have at least one foot inside the hula hoop. Too slow—or too stubborn—dogs are eliminated. Continue musical rounds until there is only one person-dog team left.

Rainy Day Games

When it's raining outside or the snow is knee-high to a St. Bernard, be a good foul-weather friend to your dog by playing games indoors. Pick a room with enough space for tail-wagging romps and stash the breakables out of paw's reach. Intermingle tricks and games with a few reinforcing obedience commands and you'll have a fun-loving dog with good manners.

Houdini Hound
EASY 🦴

HOW TO PLAY: Teach your dog to behave like a Houdini hound. Hold a small treat or ball in one closed fist and keep the other fist empty. Extend both arms out and ask your dog, "Which hand?" Let her sniff both. When she noses the fist with the toy or food, open it, show her and praise her. Repeat, randomly moving the toy or food into your left or right hand.

I Hide-You-Seek
EASY 🦴

HOW TO PLAY: Play hide and seek. Have your dog heel by your side in a room. Throw a treat across the room. As your dog darts after it, slip around the corner out of sight and call your dog by name. When she races to you, reward her with a treat and plenty of praise. Repeat four or five times. Or have her sit and stay in one room while you hide in another. Call her to come find you.

Find the Keys
MEDIUM 🦴🦴

HOW TO PLAY: Show your dog your keychain. Then stash the keychain on the couch, under a chair, or in your dog's bed. Say, "Find the keychain." When she brings it to you, reward her with a treat. Then stash it in a new place and repeat the retrieve-and-get-a-treat steps.

When the Rain Stops

Many dogs enjoy being able to romp leash-free outdoors. That explains the rising popularity of fenced-in dog parks all over the globe. Of course, certain rules apply to make the dog park a fun—and safe—place for all. Among some common rules to heed are:

🐾 Make sure your dog has up-to-date vaccinations, is healthy, and is wearing identification tags.

🐾 Leave puppies at home until they've had all their puppy shots and have demonstrated the ability to obey the commands "Sit," "Stay," and "Come."

🐾 Keep an eye on your dog at all times and never detach the leash until you've reached the designated off-leash area.

🐾 Bring water (most places provide drinking fountains at dog-eye levels) but leave food in your car. This is a playground for dogs, not a picnic area.

🐾 Keep aggressive dogs leashed—or better yet, leave them at home to avoid a dog fight.

🐾 Bring your pooper-scooper and plastic bags just in case the park doesn't provide them.

🐾 Never bring more dogs from your household than you can control. The maximum is two or three, depending on how well behaved they are and how well they stick together.

CHAPTER 10

Travel

Travel Preparations

Did someone say road trip? A popular trend, especially among empty nesters and Baby Boomers, is to travel with their dogs. When you travel, you might even purposely select a vehicle with canine amenities.

Bringing out the suitcase often causes many dogs to unleash full-body wiggles at the anticipation of joining their favorite people for a travel adventure. Where or for how long doesn't matter to them—they are just excited to be your travel mate.

What to Pack

For road trips, you may be surprised to discover that your dog's travel needs exceed what you need to bring for yourself. Keep this dog travel checklist handy to review for your next adventure on the road with your canine chum.

- Extra leash
- Extra collar
- Spare identification tags containing your cell phone number
- Pet first-aid kit
- Collapsible water and food bowls
- Pet food and treats
- Two of your dog's favorite toys
- Disposable poop bags
- Doggy bed
- Blanket
- Copy of his medical record
- A muzzle (in case your dog is injured and you need to safely restrain him)
- Bottled water
- Photo of you with your dog stashed in the glove compartment and on your cell phone
- Harness and safety restraint or a carrier with your dog inside
- Contact information, including your veterinarian, your information, and a backup person's phone number
- A minimum of one week's supply of medications and supplements
- Grooming tools, including brush, comb and lint removal product
- Cleaning items, including paper towels, moist towelettes, and enzymatic stain and odor removers
- A flat sheet to place over the hotel bed
- Flashlight

If you travel frequently with your dog, you may want to invest in rubberized floor liners and waterproof seat covers, available at auto product retailers.

Safe Driving

Accidents can happen to anyone at any time. I share this as a reminder of keeping our pets as safe as possible when they ride with us in our vehicles. Show how much you really love your dogs—and other traveling pets—by keeping them safe when you drive.

PARK YOUR PET WHILE YOU DRIVE.

Do not allow your dog to ride in the front passenger seat or in your lap or allow him to stick his head out the window. An unrestrained 60 lb dog becomes a 2,700 lb projectile in a sudden stop or an accident at 35 mph. He can generate an impact force against the windshield, seat back, or another passenger.

INVEST IN A SAFETY HARNESS.

Depending on the size of your dog, fit him in a pet safety harness securely clipped into a seatbelt in the middle seats or place him inside a pet carrier, also fastened in place.

ATTACH A LEASH.

Make sure you attach a leash to your dog before letting him out of the car to prevent escapes or accidents.

BEAT THE HEAT.

Attach a crate fan to help keep your pet cool during the drive. Freeze a couple of gallon (4.5 l) jugs of water and position them so your pet can curl up around them to keep cool—instant air conditioning! Senior dogs and canines with flat faces or short noses (such as pugs and bulldogs) can quickly succumb to heat extremes.

AVOID LETTING YOUR DOG STICK HIS HEAD OUT OF THE CAR WINDOW.

Flying debris can easily injure his eyes. Crack the window only enough to keep the air flowing. If your dog insists on poking his head out the window, strap on some safety goggles. He will then truly look the part of copilot!

CHECK FOR DROOL.

Excessive drooling is a sure sign that your dog is beginning to suffer car sickness. Park at a safe place and walk him for 5 or 10 minutes.

Pet-Friendly Hotel Stays

In the competitive world of hotel lodging, savvy hotel chains are recognizing the value of putting out the welcome mat for well-mannered dogs. Some even offer dog beds and treats in rooms.

Lodgings in all price ranges are responding to the growing trend of people traveling with their dogs and other pets. Follow these tips to guarantee that the hotel staff will put out the welcome mat.

HIT THE INTERNET BEFORE YOU HIT THE ROAD.

With the popularity of pets joining their people on road trips, there are more pet travel websites that offer details on pet-welcoming hotels and their specific pet policies. Be sure to seek unbiased comments from travelers.

HEED THE HOTEL RULES.

Some hotels prohibit leaving pets in your hotel room unsupervised. Budget to include paying for a dog walker or doggy day care for times you will be out and about without your pet.

PACK PET AMENITIES.

To help your dog feel more at home inside the hotel room, be sure to bring familiar items bearing his scent, such as his bed or his favorite toy.

BOTTLED WATER ONLY.

Travel can cause gastrointestinal upset in some pets, so stick with bottled water and his brand of pet food during your hotel stays.

BRING ID.

Always carry a copy of your dog's health records with you, including ID cards with his photo. Some smart phone apps allow you to download these documents so you always have them available. Make sure your pet has been microchipped and that his collar tag sports your cell phone number. Some hotels also add temporary tags bearing their phone number during your stay.

SNIFF OUT NEARBY PET PLACES.

Before booking a hotel, find out the contact info on the nearest emergency vet clinic, including directions from the hotel. Also consult the hotel's concierge staff about professional pet sitters and dog walkers and dog-welcoming outdoor cafés.

PLAY IT SAFE.

Pack a pet first-aid kit in your luggage and enroll in a veterinarian-approved pet first-aid class before your trip.

SPEAK UP FOR SPECIAL ROOMS.

Request a wheelchair-accessible room if available, because the bathrooms are larger and more spacious—providing ample space for your traveling dog to snooze and stay safe without escaping. Put something under the bed to prevent small dogs from crawling under and being out of your reach.

Dining with Canines

There is a growing trend across the globe to permit leashed dogs in outdoor areas of restaurants with some savvy eating establishments catering to canine guests with special doggy menus. But the sign, "No dogs allowed" can be quickly posted if owners of these eateries must contend with rude, pushy or barking four-legged customers. To ensure your dog brings his best table manners, first do a candid assessment of his social skills. Questions to ask yourself:

🐾 Does he walk nicely on a leash?

🐾 Does he sit or hold a stay on cue?

🐾 Does he enjoy mingling with people—and other leashed dogs—in a small, confined setting like an outdoor café?

If you answered no to any of these questions, your dog may be better left in the comforts of your home while you eat at a restaurant. Not all dogs are dine-out dogs and that is okay. But if you answered yes to the above questions, then your dining experience can be pleasant and peaceful. There are some rules to abide by.

WALK OR RUN YOUR DOG FIRST.

Treat your dog to a form of aerobic exercise before you head for the café. He is more apt to be tired and nap under the table while you dine.

PICK OFF-PEAK HOURS.

Avoid the lunch or dinner rush hour to minimize canine chaos. You increase your chances of landing a better table.

SCOPE OUT THE SCENE BEFORE SITTING DOWN.

Request to be seated in a corner or away from the patio's entrance to minimize your dog from barking or wanting to rudely sniff other patrons and their dogs. Keep your dog from being overheated by finding a table that offers shade and bring a portable water bowl.

PACK A LUNCH FOR YOUR DOG.

If the restaurant does not have a doggy menu, bring your dog a healthy treat and portable collapsible water bowl.

REIN IN YOUR DOG.

To prevent your four-legged friend from begging or bothering patrons at neighboring tables, please keep him on a short leash—4 ft or 6 ft (1.2 m or 1.8 m)—and definitely, do not tether him to a retractable leash.

Dog Parks

Dog parks represent the canine versions of coffee houses. The enclosed areas are designed to serve as safe places for dogs to socialize, unleash pent-up energy, and enjoy leash-free roaming and romping with dog-friendly canines.

Will your dog enjoy being at a dog park? Assess your dog's attitude. Some crave canine companionship; some focus solely on chasing tennis balls and couldn't care less if there are other dogs in the park; whereas others prefer hanging out with people.

Make sure your dog heeds both vocal cues and hand signals from you consistently. He should heed "Watch me," "Come" and "Stay" to keep him safe inside a dog park. Knowing hand signals is key if the park is filled with barking dogs and you are far from your dog and need to communicate with him. No matter if you plan to take your dog to his regular park or make a first-time visit to one, it is advised to show some precautions beforehand. Recognize that there are risks involved when you turn loose a large number of dogs who don't know each other. If the dogs do not have good recall (come when they are called) and owners are not paying attention, there is a serious risk of dogs getting into fights and being injured.

BEFORE YOUR VISIT TO THE PARK
STUDY THE MOODS OF PARK DOGS.
Spend a few moments watching the interactions before entering the park. Study the "mood" of the dogs inside. Happy dogs tend to sport smiling open mouths, do play bows and have relaxed bodies. Aggressive dogs tend to lean forward on their toes, keep their mouths tightly shut or snarl, stare intently and have stiff postures.

PREDICT POTENTIAL DOG FIGHTS.
Nix the dog park if you witness canine fights or notice that people inside are not paying attention to their dogs. Keep your dog safe by taking him to another park or on a long walk instead.

DON'T BRING FOOD.

Avoid bringing in food for you or treats for your dog. You risk attracting other dogs who may get into a food fight or who may have allergies to certain foods.

LEAVE FAVORITE TOYS AT HOME.

Other dogs may "steal" or destroy your dog's favorite toy. Avoid any resource-guarding issues.

DON'T BRING YOUNG KIDS.

Do not bring toddlers or young children inside a dog park. At their heights, they may be staring eye-to-eye with a dog, a canine threat gesture. Also, toddlers are unsure on their feet and can accidentally trip and fall into a dog, who may respond with a reactive bite.

ENSURE YOUR DOG IS VACCINATED.

Bring dogs who are up-to-date on their vaccinations, heartworm medications and flea/tick preventives. No one wants canine cooties!

ENTER THE DOG PARK WITH CONFIDENCE.

Time your dog's entrance when there are not a lot of dogs hovering at the gate. Bunched-up dogs in a tight space triggers the fight-or-flight response. Speak in an upbeat tone as you encourage your dog to "Go play."

Find others with well-mannered dogs and organize times to meet at your favorite dog park. Your dogs will enjoy these happy reunions and romp with unbridled joy.

AT THE PARK
CLEAN UP AFTER YOUR DOG.

Pick up your dog's "deposits" without being told by another park attendee.

PAY ATTENTION.

Don't become distracted with cell phone calls or camp out in the corner of the park to read a book or newspaper. Pay attention to your dog's actions and be ready to intervene before an encounter escalates into a fight.

DON'T PANIC.

Watch in silence as your dog mingles. Don't panic if one dog puts his head over the back of another. They are just determining who is top dog. Don't gasp or shriek if one dog's hackles are raised. In some breeds, like Siberian Huskies, raised hair on the back happens automatically whenever they are stimulated.

SOME DOGS YAP TO CHAT.

Some dogs like to yap during an intro, especially vocal breeds like Schnauzers or Beagles. There may be a quick verbal exchange in what I describe as "canine air guitar." Often, it ends quickly and the two will play or choose to go in different directions. If you sense an escalated exchange, direct your dog to join you in another area of the park.

KEEP DOG LEASHES ON HAND.

Never slack your dog's leash in case a meet-and-greet erupts into a brawl. If a brawl occurs, speak in a low, commanding tone to both dogs to "Knock it off!" or "Leave it!" Resist the temptation to grab your dog's collar because you risk being bitten. Instead, loop the leash over your dog's chest and pull the dogs apart. Assess for any injuries and leave.

Hikes

Want to take the ho-hum out of your daily dog walks plus treat your dog to new sights, sounds and smells? Seeking a great workout for the both of you? Well, take a hike.

Hiking offers many benefits—a cardiovascular workout, the chance to explore new places, a healthy outlet to combat stress and much more. Before you lace up your hiking boots and connect your dog's leash to his buckle collar or harness, you need to know how to make your hike a fun and safe adventure.

BOOK A SNOUT-TO-TAIL PHYSICAL EXAMINATION.
Bring your dog to your veterinary clinic for a thorough physical examination. Your veterinarian will assess your dog's fitness, evaluate his range of motion, and alert you to any possible health concerns. Don't forget to get a physical from your physician as well.

GO DOG-LESS THE FIRST TIME.
My emergency care and sports medicine veterinarian friends emphasize the need to know the trail—and its potential hazards—before bringing your dog. You don't want to risk harm to your dog by letting him off leash to jump over a large log up ahead across the trail; maybe the trail continues safely on, or maybe there's a rock-filled ditch or deep gorge ahead.

ENSURE YOUR DOG HEEDS THE "COME BACK" CALL.
Practice your dog's recall capabilities in enclosed areas like your backyard and in dog parks before allowing him to be off-leash in hiking areas that

permit dogs on trails without being leashed. If your dog will come when called, you can get him out of just about any dangerous situation—like avoiding a cliff, rushing river, approaching a wild animal, being stung by a hive of bees or bitten by a rattlesnake. This is the single most important command a dog can learn.

BUILD SLOWLY AND AVOID "WEEKEND WARRIOR" SYNDROME.
Gradually expand the distance, duration and elevation of your daily walks until you and your dog can comfortably complete walks lasting more than 1 hour. Do not exercise with your dog only on weekends because you risk injuries to your muscles and joints. Dogs suffer muscle pain just like humans. This can be immediate or can happen a few hours later or the next day. It can be quite painful.

FACTOR IN YOUR DOG'S AGE. Dogs under age 1 are still developing their muscles and bones and should not go on hikes lasting more than half a day. Don't overtax senior dogs who may be emotionally willing but lack the physical condition to complete a long, arduous hike.

PACK WITH SAFETY AND FORTITUDE IN MIND.
Your backpack should include plenty of water for you and your dog, high-quality, easy-to-digest protein treats (such as dried liver or string cheese), power bars for you as well as a small pet first-aid kit and your cell phone.

Gradually condition your dog for longer hikes to prevent him from incurring injuries so the both of you can enjoy a trek through the countryside.

FIRST-AID CLASSES

Enroll in a veterinarian-approved pet first-aid class before going on a hike. In classes like mine, you learn what to do—and what not to do—in a pet emergency when minutes count. Learn how to use what you have in your gear to treat bee stings, cut paw pads, broken legs, dehydration and much more.

CHAPTER 11
Canine Sports

Keeping Your Dog Athletic

Your best workout buddy can be a four-legged jock. Watching a happy, healthy, agile dog is a sight to behold and to admire, so spend quality time ensuring that your dog gets appropriate and varied levels of exercise.

Meet one of the fastest growing dog breeds: the canine athlete. More dogs of all shapes and sizes are running, jumping, herding, fetching and competing in a variety of sports than ever before. But whether your dog's workout consists of taking brisk daily walks or wowing packed arenas with her disk-catching prowess, she needs proper conditioning to stave off injury and deliver peak performances.

BOOK A WELLNESS VETERINARY VISIT.

Before you begin your dog in any athletic activity, have your veterinarian perform a complete physical examination. And, if your dog is say, 6 years or older, a complete blood work up is recommended. You want to make sure that there is no organ dysfunction that may hinder athletic performance.

WATCH YOUR DOG'S WEIGHT.

Canine athletes perform best when they are at their ideal body weights. A few extra pounds can add unwanted stress to a dog's joints and muscles and may trigger injuries. Work with your veterinarian on pinpointing your dog's daily calorie need.

PAY ATTENTION TO THE WEATHER.

Dogs are closer to the sidewalk and wooded trail and thus are more exposed to heat and humidity than people are. Look for early warning signs of heat exhaustion—such as a slowing pace, stopping, heavy panting and a wide, flattened tongue. (See box for other signs.)

Be careful not to overtax your dog during athletic activities. You need to know when to end any session before he overtires.

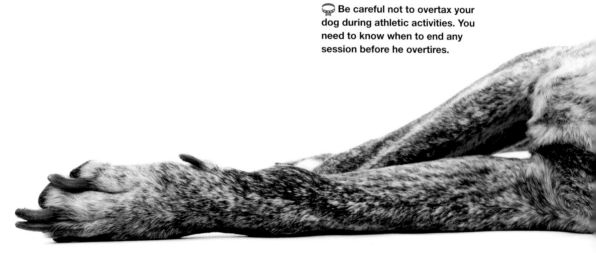

VARY YOUR DOG'S WORKOUT ROUTINE.

Even though your dog may be an ace at agility, her body will benefit by the chance to mix it up with diverse types of exercise. Perhaps train your dog to use a treadmill, learn to swim in safe waters, and hone her fetching skills.

AVOID WEEKEND WARRIOR SYNDROME.

Dogs need proper stretching routines and to engage in regular exercise year-round. Injuries are more apt to occur in a dog who lounges on the sofa during the week and then spends the weekend performing in agility or other potentially exhausting sports. They need to be gradually conditioned to the specific demands of the activities they enjoy.

The following pages offer up suggestions to inspire you to help find your dog engaging and energetic types of exercise.

DOG-TIRED SIGNS

Be careful not to overexert your dog in canine sports or during training sessions. If your dog displays any of the following signs, stop the activity and allow her to rest:

- Drooping tongue that is bright red.
- Rapid panting—an early sign of overheating.
- Hesitation. Notice if your dog is starting to take a few extra seconds before retrieving a tossed ball.
- Weight shifting. Determine if your dog is starting to use different muscle groups to offset soreness.
- Staggered walking.
- Muscle tremors.
- Limping. Check footpads for cuts and bruises and legs for sprains or muscle pulls.

Dog Agility

Many dogs do more than fetch, run or play tug-of-war. They are bow-wowing crowds in a growing list of organized canine sports all over the globe. First up is agility training.

Agility can build a dog's confidence, while providing a great workout, both physically and mentally. Train or compete as a team by guiding your unleashed dog through an obstacle course. Teach your dog to jump hurdles and scale ramps. Show her how to crawl through tunnels, weave in and out of poles and balance on the teeter board. Agility is a sport that can be enjoyed on various levels by dogs and their people. You work together with your dog heeding your voice and hand signal instructions to negotiate a course of obstacles as quickly as possible. The clock starts when your dog leaves the start line and ends when she finishes the arena full of obstacles. The training is about having fun with your dog—whether practicing in your backyard or with an organized club. It can be addictive and many participants go on to enter local competitions.

Find an agility club with experienced instructors and equipment that meets safety criteria. Look for a small beginner's class, with dogs who are similar in size to yours. Avoid large classes because you will get less individualized attention.

Rules

Agility is a sport for dogs of all breeds and sizes. Classes and trials are categorized by a dog's size and ability level. Canine participants must be unleashed and their owners (or designated handlers) can communicate through hand signals or verbal commands only. They may not touch their dogs or the equipment on the course. Judging is based on the dog's speed and accuracy to complete the obstacles in a set sequence. "Faults" are given when a dog performs incorrectly or out of sequence.

The Course and Obstacles

Course configurations vary, as do the obstacles, depending on the sponsoring organization. These courses are designed for the dogs' level of experience and height category—smaller dogs have shorter jumps, for example.

CONTACT OBSTACLES

The A-frame, dog walk, teeter boards (seesaw) and tunnel obstacles have yellow "contact zones" at each end. Dogs must get at least one paw into these zones when mounting or dismounting the obstacle.

JUMP OBSTACLES

Dogs jump over horizontal bars, over or across a solid panel, and through a suspended tire or circular ring.

OTHER OBSTACLES

Weave poles are upright poles spaced apart that dogs navigate through. The flat table (or pause table) is a square platform onto which the dog must jump and pause in a sit or a down until given a verbal or hand signal to jump off.

Age

 You can start teaching your puppy many of the agility skills, such as basic obedience commands, at a young age. However, it is best to introduce obstacles after the puppy is 1 year of age. To jump and weave in agility, your dog will need the strength and coordination that comes with full maturity. Although it is different for each dog, at 1 year old most dogs have finished growing. They are then able to perform safely on the equipment and have the attention span necessary to heed instructions to complete the obstacles.

Older dogs may also take part. Their joints may be weaker and they may tire more easily, but the right class will take that into consideration. As long as the dog is physically healthy, age doesn't prevent her from participating in agility training or competition.

Requirements

All your dog needs is energy, and an understanding of the basic obedience commands. Don't worry if your dog is new to the "sit," "stay," "come" and "down" commands, because agility training will help to reinforce them. Agility is a fast-paced sport as well as a social sport. Make sure your dog is comfortable around strangers and other dogs before considering this sport.

Fetching Sports

Dogs love chasing balls, but have you tried throwing a frisbee? Popular for decades, the sport of frisbee or canine flying disk continues to grow in the number of canine participants and tricks.

Got a dog who cons you into marathon games of fetch? You just may have an athlete in the making. Canines competing in the fast-growing disk dog sport thrive on running super fast, making hairpin turns and acrobatically soaring and snatching a flying disk in mid-air. This sport, answering to such names as disk dogs, canine disk, frisbee flying disk and more, is best suited for speedy dogs who love to show off and always keep their eyes on the prize: in this case, an airborne disk whose flight pattern is determined by the toss of the handler and wind conditions.

WATER-BASED ACTIVITIES

Some dogs like to make a splash. Whether it is a simple act of fetching a floatable toy in the ocean or lake, or the complex skill of flying off a dock into a body of water. If the latter, you might like to try your dog out with a fast-growing canine sport: dock diving. This is a fun, active sport that gives dogs the chance to swim, run and jump and get their adrenalin pumping. The appeal is global with events hosted in the United States, Canada, Australia and the United Kingdom.

Play it safe by always fitting your dog with a canine life vest to keep him safe in the water. Especially one with a the handle on top for easy grabbing.

Frisbee Training

Generate interest in this sport to your dog by flipping the disk over and using it as a food bowl initially. Before mealtime, playfully kick the upside-down disk on the kitchen floor and encourage your dog to retrieve it. Then roll the disk on the floor for your dog to chase, grab and retrieve. If your dog shows keen interest, then you are ready to head outside in an enclosed area.

To be both successful and safe, you need to slowly build on each step and slowly increase the distance of the throw. In this sport, dogs need to know how to run, track and catch. Practice sessions are designed to teach dogs to follow the flight of the Frisbee and make the adjustment when the Frisbee makes a slight tilt in the air to the left or right.

Your athletic dog will develop self confidence and keep in shape by participating in this sport.

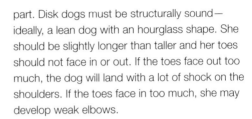

Is Your Dog a Disk Dog?

Dogs with strong prey drives, prey chase and prey kill do well in this sport when properly trained to re-channel those natural instincts. Although herding dogs like Border Collies are often seen in the disk dog arena, many mixed breeds also do well but body build does play a key part. Disk dogs must be structurally sound — ideally, a lean dog with an hourglass shape. She should be slightly longer than taller and her toes should not face in or out. If the toes face out too much, the dog will land with a lot of shock on the shoulders. If the toes face in too much, she may develop weak elbows.

Because this sport requires dogs to run, leap high in the air and turn quickly, it is not conducive for breeds with long backs and short legs, such as Corgis and Dachshunds. Nor does it beckon heavy, slow-moving breeds like Bulldogs. Age is also considered. Most disk dog organizations heed the "18-month rule" and set that as the minimum age for a dog to compete so that ample time is given for her growth plates to fully close.

There are two primary competition formats — toss-and-fetch and freestyle.

TOSS-AND-FETCH.

Don't blink or you may miss the action in the toss-and-fetch format. Dogs line up behind a line and the handler has a stack of disks. Top points go to the dog who catches the most disks in 90 seconds in the greatest distance — usually 40 yards (36 m).

FREESTYLE.

The freestyle format features choreographed musical routines where dog and handler are judged for execution, creativity and covering most of the field. Think of this as a cross between figure skating and gymnastics — only for dogs. Each high-energy routine lasts between 90 seconds and 3 minutes. Look for spectacular vaults, mid-air catches, flips and a tricky maneuver called the Dog Catch where the person must catch their dog in their arms just as the dog snares the disk in the air.

Musical Freestyle

Consider harmonizing with your dog, really harmonizing, set to music. Canine musical freestyle is an energetic, crowd-pleasing sport that incorporates basic and advanced obedience cues to music.

Love to dance? Got a dog who enjoys joining you in a cha cha? Millions tune in each season to watch two-legged celebrities compete on popular dance shows, such as "Dancing with the Stars." But also drawing applause are sanctioned canine dance competitions where the partners consist of a person and a dog. There is the increased possibility of missteps and a team having three left feet. Canine musical freestyle is also known as heelwork to music, paws 2 dance and other names. Regardless of the name dubbed by the sanctioning organization, this musical choreographed sport scores a hit with participants and attendees.

Got a dog who loves to walk on her hind legs and weave between your legs? She would make an ideal participant in musical freestyle.

Unlike in conventional canine sports like agility, obedience or rally trials that require participants to do the same thing, canine musical freestyle offers you and your dog the opportunity to entertain and really touch the hearts of people and make them laugh, cry and feel something. Some of the best dance duos require dogs to perform left side heels, hind leg raises, weaves, spins and other maneuvers choreographed to music.

This is a team sport that welcomes people and dogs of all ages and abilities. The key to success is how well your dog pays attention to your hand signals and subtle body cues and her willingness to perform in front of an audience.

Musical Freestyle
Steps to Success

Master the basics first. Enroll your dog in a basic obedience class that incorporates positive reinforcement techniques.

INCORPORATE CLICKER TRAINING.

Some of the most successful dancing dogs learn specific moves "marked" by the sound of the clicker during training sessions.

PLAY IT SAFE.

Don't start your puppy at too young of an age and don't risk injuries to her limbs by requiring her to rise up and balance on her hind legs for longer than a few seconds.

MAKE IT FUN.

Not all dogs are born dancers. Don't force your dog to dance and never become impatient during training sessions. Some routines can take a few months to perfect.

BE FLEXIBLE.

Some dogs love to improvise during competition, so it takes a savvy dance partner to be able to adapt when a dog makes an unexpected move. Scoring is based on the interaction of the team and the ability to incorporate various moves.

SHINE THE SPOTLIGHT
ON YOUR CANINE PARTNER.

Don't let your outfit, props or dance moves be distractive and take away from your dog's performance. You won't score points with judges.

AGE IS NOT A FACTOR.

In recent years, dog dance groups have added divisions answering to names like Sassy Seniors, which welcome grey-muzzled dogs and people in their golden years.

DO YOUR OWN THING.

You and your dog will make a unique team. Test out different music to see what makes your dog's tail go up. Dogs have a definite affinity to certain music. And most of all have fun communicating and socializing with your dog. Dancing is one of the most wonderful ways to bond with your dog.

This sport gives you the opportunity to unleash your creativity and communicate with your dog in a fun way.

CHAPTER 12
Pet First Aid

First Aid Preparation

What happens if your dog cuts his paw, gets stung by a bee or, worse, he chokes on a chew toy, collapses and stops breathing? These are just a few reasons why you should learn pet first aid.

We can spoil our dogs with stays in pet-welcoming hotels or lavish them with designer pet beds or custom-fitted outfits. But knowing how to stabilize and immobilize your dog in a pet emergency so you can get him safely to your veterinarian is worth far more than showering your pet with the latest outfit, designer bowl or toy. Give your dog the priceless gift by enrolling in a pet first-aid class where you will learn what to do—and more importantly, what not to do—in a pet emergency, when minutes count. After all, pets don't live in protective bubbles, but you can reduce your dog's risk for injuries and medical emergencies by taking a proactive, preventive stance.

Actions and Attitudes That Could Save Your Dog's Life

Nothing beats the value of participating in a pet first-aid class firsthand in a classroom. But in this chapter, we will offer you some pet first-aid tips and tricks to inspire you. Ready to be your dog's best health ally? Let's begin!

KNOW WHAT'S NORMAL FOR YOUR DOG.

Once a month, perform a thorough head-to-tail wellness assessment of your dog. By looking, listening and smelling, you can often catch early signs of illness or injury, which could be treated more completely and less expensively by a vet. The added bonus is that your dog becomes more comfortable when being touched, making him more cooperative around veterinarians, pet sitters, dog walkers, groomers and other pet professionals.

STOP AND COLLECT YOURSELF BEFORE APPROACHING AN INJURED DOG.

Resist rushing up to your canine because you risk being bitten. Instead, stop, take a deep breath in and exhale, and survey the scene to make sure you are safe.

PRACTICE PLAYFUL MUZZLING SESSIONS WITH YOUR DOG.

When your canine pal is happy and healthy, use treats and praise as you hone your skills on wrapping him in a bath towel or putting on a safety muzzle. Remember, even the sweetest dog in the world can bite and claw you when injured and in pain. By practicing the proper way to safely restrain your dog when he is healthy, you gain confidence and your pet makes a positive association of the restraint with a tasty reward.

DON'T PANIC WHEN YOUR PET IS IN PAIN.

Pets tap into our emotional moods and that is why it is vital not to scream or rush up to your injured dog, especially if he is choking. Your emotional outburst could cause your dog to try to flee or rush to swallow an item and start to choke.

DON'T PLAY VETERINARIAN.

Whenever possible in a pet emergency, put your phone on speaker mode and call your veterinarian for guidance. For instance, your veterinarian may advise you to immediately induce vomiting in your dog if he ate rat bait by using hydrogen peroxide.

FIRST-AID KIT

Keep a large pet first-aid kit in your home and a smaller version in your vehicle. Always examine the contents inside the kit twice a year and replace any item that has become outdated. Stock your kit with:

- Plastic syringe
- Tweezers
- Blunt-end scissors
- Eye dropper
- Digital thermometer
- Gauze rolls
- Gauze pads
- Triangular bandages
- Self-cling bandage that stretches but does not stick to fur
- Adhesive tape
- Pet-safe antihistamine
- Antiseptic wipes
- Hydrogen peroxide
- Chemical ice pack
- Betadine solution
- Muzzle
- Spare leash and harness
- Plastic resealable bags

- Permanent marking pen and notepad
- Towel
- Non-latex disposable gloves
- Flashlight
- Cotton swabs and cotton balls
- Spare sock and sneaker shoe laces
- Wooden tongue depressors or popsicle sticks to use to splint a broken leg
- Photo of you with your dog (for easy identification verification)
- Copy of your dog's medical records and veterinary contact info stored in a waterproof bag
- Mylar emergency blanket
- Sterile saline solution
- Styptic powder

Consult with your veterinarian to find a pet first-aid class available in your area.

Towel Wrapping

Your normally sweet Shih Tzu or cuddly Chihuahua can quickly transform into a lunging, snapping, biting four-legged terror when injured and in pain. To keep you safe and maintain control of your tiny dog, turn to a surprising ally in a pet first-aid situation: a large bathroom towel. Wrapping your diminutive dog in a large towel is a good way to protect yourself because you stop his paws from scratching you and towel wrapping also prevents escapes.

Introduce the towel in a positive way. Create a positive association by placing your dog when he is healthy and happy on top of a towel and show him a small treat. Place the treat on the towel so your dog has to lie or sit on the towel to eat it.

Loosely wrap the towel over your dog's back while he eats. Gently pet his back and let him walk away when he is done eating.

1 Start with your dog several inches from the front edge of the towel and about a foot from one side.

2 Pull the front of the towel up around your dog's neck snugly so that he can't get his legs over the towel. Hold the towel ends together over the back of his neck.

3 Hold the towel together with one hand. With your free hand, wrap the towel over your dog.

4 Be sure to take up the slack on the side. There should be no room for your dog to squirm.

5 Next, wrap the other side snugly.

6 Tuck the towel in and wrap it under your dog.

7 Wrap the towel around your dog again.

8 When the wrap is snug, you should be able to lift your dog by the towel and he should look comfortable.

9 If your dog wiggles to get out the back, wrap the back of the towel up and over his hind end, or cover his rear with a second towel.

🦴 **Conscious dogs in pain need to be safely muzzled to prevent them from biting you while you perform first aid on them.**

Muzzle for Safety

To provide pet first aid to a conscious, injured dog, you need to protect yourself from being bitten. You do this by quickly applying a muzzle to your dog. There are many commercially available dog muzzles, to fit all breeds, available at pet supply stores. Make sure you keep one that fits your dog in a pet first-aid kit in your home and in your vehicle.

Naturally, canine calamities tend to occur when a pet first-aid kit is not handy. Here are some common items you can use to loop around an injured dog's muzzle to firmly shut his mouth to allow him to still breathe, but not be able to open his powerful jaws and bite you:

🐾 Shoelaces from sneakers. Select ones that are thick and made of cotton so that they will not cut into your dog's muzzle as would shoelaces from dress shoes, which tend to be narrow and coated.
🐾 A spare nylon dog leash.
🐾 Gauze roll.
🐾 Long sleeves from a sweatshirt.
🐾 Pantyhose.

Pet Emergencies

If your dog stopped breathing and his heart stopped pumping, whether he survives may depend on how quickly—and properly—you set in and perform cardiopulmonary resuscitation (CPR) and rescue breathing.

CPR

One minute your dog could be playing with a squeaker toy and the next, he could suddenly collapse and stop breathing. Or he could suffer from shock after chewing an electric cord plugged into an outlet and his heart stops beating. Or he could be struck by a vehicle. There are a variety of injuries and illnesses that can cause heart cessation in dogs.

To revive him, every minute counts. That's why knowing how to perform cardiopulmonary resuscitation can be a true life-saving skill. CPR is as easy as A, B, C. That stands for airway, breathing and circulation. You need to take action immediately, especially if the nearest veterinary clinic is 15 or 20 minutes away. Instead of spending time to try to find a pulse to determine if a dog has a heartbeat, the latest veterinarian-approved CPR protocols recommend immediately performing compressions on the pet's chest.

Upon discovering that your dog is unconscious and not breathing, CPR consists of you performing 30 chest compressions, followed by two breaths of air from your mouth directly into your dog's nose.

Repeat this 30 compressions-two-breaths-of-air sequence before checking for a pulse by placing your two middle fingers directly on your dog's femoral artery, located on the inside of his back thigh near the groin. The mindset is that there is enough oxygen in the tissue and bloodstream with compressions of the chest circulating that oxygen.

Also, evidence shows that every time you stop compressions, you decrease the chance of survival.

If you witness your dog collapse and stop breathing, first collect yourself by inhaling and exhaling. This helps you not to panic and to focus on the emergency situation. Next, survey the scene to make sure it is safe to reach your dog, especially if you are outside near traffic. Depending on the size of your dog, you will need to perform the compressions in one of three methods:

🐾 Taco CPR
🐾 Side-to-side CPR
🐾 Barrel-chested CPR

All three follow the sequence of 30 compressions with two breaths of air times two. The difference is where you place your hands for performing the compressions.

Taco CPR Method

This type of CPR is performed on small dogs and puppies that you can easily cradle in one arm like an infant.

1 Place your fingers on your small dog's chest in the space between his two front legs.

2 Use your fingers to compress the dog's chest one-third to one-fourth in width in a steady, quick pace for 30 counts.

3 Tilt the dog's head back to open his airway.

4 Gently pull his tongue forward past his canine teeth for greater airway opening.

5 Close his mouth by cupping your hands on each side of his face to form an airtight seal.

6 Give two steady breaths of air from your mouth directly into your dog's nostrils. You should see his chest rising and falling.

7 Give a second set of 30 compressions followed by two breaths of air before assessing for a heartbeat by checking for a pulse on his femoral artery.

Side-To-Side CPR Method

This type of CPR is the most common type performed on a majority of dogs who are too big to hold in your arm and do not have broad, expansive chests. Examples include Cairn Terriers, Miniature Schnauzers, Labrador Retrievers and Siberian Huskies. Your unconscious, non-breathing dog will be on his side. Dogs can collapse on either their left or their right sides but the below sequence is based on a dog lying on their right side—alternate hand positioning if your dog is on his left side.

1 Kneel at your dog's spine.

2 Place the open palm of your left hand on your dog's chest. Tuck your thumb under your dog's front armpit and ensure your palm is parallel and facing the floor.

3 With your right hand, tilt your dog's head to open his airway.

4 With your right hand, form a fist. Position your arm so your fist is anchored against your dog's stomach. This keeps your dog from moving.

5 With your open palm on the chest, begin 30 chest compressions.

6 Then give two breaths of air. Repeat the 30 compressions and two breaths of air.

7 Check for a pulse on his femoral artery.

Barrel-Chested CPR Method

This type of CPR is performed on breeds with big, broad chests, such as Bulldogs, Pugs and Bull Mastiffs. These dogs are able to easily sleep belly-up because their wide shoulders balance their backs on the ground.

1 Kneel close to your dog.

2 If he is on one side, position both hands over the belly and between the top front and top back leg. Grab the bottom front and back legs to bring your dog to a belly-up position.

3 Cross your open palms over your dog's heart (located in the space between his front elbows on his chest).

4 Deliver 30 chest compressions, followed by two breaths of air. Repeat this sequence.

5 Check for a pulse on his femoral artery.

Heed the instructions given to you by your veterinarian by phone if your dog suffers from severe bleeding.

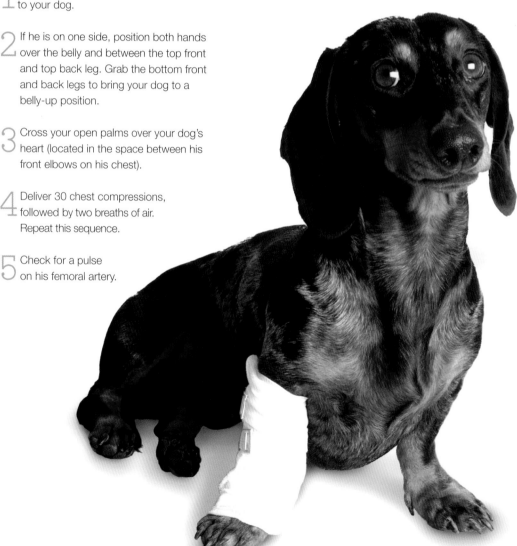

Stop the Bleeding

If your dog steps on broken glass, catches his dewclaw in the carpet or has his ear bitten in a dogfight, expect blood to flow. At times like these you need to know the steps to slow or stop the bleeding and take your dog to the nearest veterinary clinic. A laceration of a large artery or vein could lead to life-threatening bleeding in minutes. The likelihood of a dog's "bleeding out" depends on how quickly he's treated and the type of bleeding that has occurred. The three types are:

- Arterial, characterized by spurting, bright red blood.
- Venous, characterized by a slower flow of dark-red blood.
- Capillary, characterized by superficial blood oozing, as could occur from a nick in the tip of the ear.

EMERGENCY HELP

Seek assistance by calling for help. Have an individual call the nearest veterinary clinic to alert them of your arrival so that they can advise you and prepare an exam room. If you are alone, use the speakerphone option on your phone to make the call to the veterinary clinic so that you can continue to perform CPR. Certainly, there are some limitations after a pet emergency as to what an owner can do, but knowing pet first aid is very important. An ounce of prevention goes a long way. Pet-proof your home so that you can keep potential dangers out of access to your dog.

Act quickly because once a dog has lost more than 30 percent of blood volume, he begins to develop serious shock. The first step is to protect yourself, by restraining and muzzling your dog quickly. Keep a dog muzzle in your pet first-aid kit at home and one in your car. Even the sweetest family pet may bite when he is distressed and in pain from a bleeding laceration; it is best to be cautious and use a muzzle. The next step is to apply direct pressure on the wound by using sterile gauze pads from a first-aid kit. If no sterile gauze is available, a clean towel, T-shirt or any clean fabric available will work.

If blood saturates the first layer of gauze or clothing, apply another clean layer on top and apply direct pressure. Do not remove the first layer because the blood is clotting. You may need to apply several layers and direct pressure to slow or stop the bleeding. Then wrap roll gauze or fabric at least two or three times around the wound and secure it with medical tape. Be careful to make the wrap snug but not so tight that it will cut off circulation.

As soon as possible, call the nearest veterinary clinic to let them know you're on your way so that the staff can prepare a room for your dog. Ideally, have a family member or friend drive while you limit your dog's movements in the vehicle, try to keep him calm, and monitor him for signs of shock. Signs of shock include pale gums, a fast heart rate and weak pulses. Depending on the severity of the injury, your dog may be given pain medication and stitches. He may require follow-up visits for new wound dressings.

The Buzz on Treating Bee Stings

Dogs, even pampered ones who rarely venture beyond fenced backyards, are never completely safe from being stung by venomous insects. All it takes is for a wayward bee or wasp to slip through an open door or window and catch your dog's attention. His innate prey drive kicks into gear as he leaps and attempts to swat and eat the flying insect.

Most bee or wasp stings occur on a dog's front paw or face. If your dog gets stung, don't panic. In most instances, there will be mild swelling or tenderness in the area where your dog was stung. If the sting site is swollen and a little puffy, it is considered a localized reaction to the sting. For mild reactions, your first step is to try to remove the stinger as quickly as possible to slow down the spread of the venom in your dog's body. Keep in mind that the stinger can pump venom into a dog for up to 3 minutes after being separated from the bee. If the stinger is visible in the coat, use a credit card to scrape it out. Never attempt to squeeze the stinger out with tweezers because the venom sac may rupture, further exposing your dog to more venom. Try to keep your dog quiet and calm and apply cool compresses to the sting site to reduce mild swelling. Run a washcloth under some cool tap water; wring it out of excess water before placing it on the paw or face. Do not use icy cold compresses or ice wrapped in a towel because they can cause your dog to shiver—stick with cool compresses.

Monitor your dog and contact your local veterinarian if the swelling grows and spreads. Most likely, the veterinarian will advise you to give an over-the-counter antihistamine, such as Benadryl. Keep the medication in your pet first-aid kit to be prepared for such an emergency. Select a product that only contains one ingredient: diphenhydramine. In general, the maximum dose for dogs is 1 mg per 1 lb (0.5 kg) of body weight, but find out the correct dose amount to administer to your dog from your veterinarian.

Some dogs, just like people, are extremely allergic to insect bites. The areas around the sting site balloon in size. Within 5 to 10 minutes, their gums go from pink to white; they start vomiting; begin having difficulty breathing; start to drool; act confused and may go into anaphylactic shock. They can die if they do not receive immediate veterinary care.

Cool Advice for Burns

Your always-investigating canine can be at risk for one of three types of burns: chemical, electrical and thermal. He could ingest pool chemicals, chew on an exposed electrical cord, or burn his front paws on a hot stove. And, just like people, dogs can suffer first-, second- or third-degree burns. First-degree burns cause mild discomfort; second-degree burns penetrate several skin layers and are very painful; and third-degree burns injure all layers of the skin and can cause shock in your dog. If your dog becomes burned, take these three steps:

1 Quickly restrain your dog with a muzzle or large bath towel. Be careful not to wrap him too tightly in the towel because he can overheat en route to the veterinary clinic.

2 Gently place a damp cloth soaked in cool clean water on the burn site. This will act as a compress to help take away some of the heat from the burn site.

3 Call the nearest veterinary clinic to let them know you are on your way so that an exam room can be ready to treat this medical emergency.

WHAT NOT TO DO:

* Use ice cubes on the burn site because you risk your dog developing hypothermia.
* Apply a gauze pad or wrap on the burn site because gauze can disrupt a blister if one forms.
* Pour lemon juice or vinegar to try to neutralize a chemical burn. Unintentionally, you are producing heat and causing more tissue damage.
* Use over-the-counter burn ointments formulated for people on the burn site because some dogs are sensitive to ingredients in products made for humans.

BURN PREVENTION

To reduce the risk of your dog incurring a burn, heed these safety strategies:

* Place electrical cords inside chew-resistant casings, especially if you have a puppy or young adult dog keen on exploring his surroundings.
* Usher dogs into an enclosed room with toys and treats or a canine kennel while you prepare meals and wait to welcome them out until the stovetop has cooled.
* Switch from flame candles to battery-operated ones that flicker but do not emit heat.
* Store all chemicals in storage areas that pets and children can't access.
* Position a fireplace screen to block your dog's access to wood- or gas-burning firerplaces. The screen also keeps hot cinders from flying out.

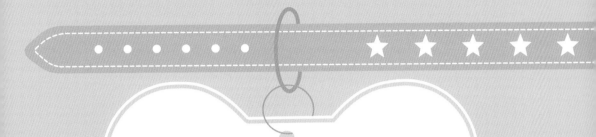

CHAPTER 13

Budgeting

Money Matters

There is no such thing as a free dog. Even if you adopt a stray dog, you need to make sure you have money to provide your dog with food, veterinary care, bedding, toys and other pet-related necessities.

Arguably, our most priceless asset is our pets. The unconditional love and devotion dogs deliver to us simply cannot be measured by any monetary value. But unless you live with a canine television or movie star like Lassie or an Internet celebrity sensation like Tillman, the skateboard-and-surfboard-riding bulldog, don't expect her to become the family breadwinner any time soon. It is imperative to be smarter than ever on how we spend our money. People all over the globe are searching for ways to stretch the family budget—and that includes expenses doled out for pets.

INVEST IN QUALITY COMMERCIAL PET FOOD.

Select pet food that lists a real meat as the first ingredient—not corn meal or wheat. Doing so can keep your pet healthy and that translates into fewer vet bills to deal with pancreatitis, diabetes, and a host of other health conditions. Don't forget to sniff out store coupons or contact your favorite pet manufacturer and request coupons.

BRING OUT YOUR PET CHEF SKILLS.

Keep more money in your pocketbook by making healthy homemade treats in a large enough batch that you can store the extras in the freezer. You can use top-quality ingredients, but they will cost less because you're not paying for packaging and marketing and shipping.

ONLY USE DOG TOOTHPASTES AND BRUSHES.

Use toothpastes and brushes designed for pets. These at-home dental items are minor in cost compared to a professional dental cleaning performed at a veterinary clinic.

PACKAGE THE NECESSARY VACCINATIONS.

Consult your veterinarian about what vaccinations your dog truly needs and base it on your pet's age, health and outdoor access. Opt for 3-year vaccinations when possible instead of annual ones.

GET STORE BARGAINS.

Save a little to a lot of money by buying leashes, bowls, beds and treats at places that primarily cater to two-leggers, such as major discount retailers like Wal-Mart, Target and Costco instead of pet supply stores or pet boutiques.

BUY IN BULK.

Look for treats and chews from online pet supply catalogs and store them in the freezer until you need them. For dry food, you shouldn't really buy too much in bulk, but if you do then store it inside airtight containers to keep it fresh.

ASK ABOUT MULTIPLE PET DISCOUNTS.

Veterinarians and groomers often offer a price break on an office visit or grooming if you bring in more than one pet at a time.

SHOP AROUND AND THEN BARGAIN.

If a catalog has a low price on heartworm pills or flea treatment, ask if your veterinarian will match it.

Just remember: happy tail wags are always free and welcomed. You might lack a few of the luxuries in life, but you're never poor as long as you have the love of your dog.

FORM A BUYING CO-OP WITH PET-OWNING FRIENDS.

Lots of catalogs offer a discounted bulk price for large group orders.

TRADE YOUR SERVICES.

If you have a particular skill—writing, painting, making pottery, mowing, gardening, detailing automobiles—consider offering your talents in trade for pet services.

WORK THE WEB.

Consider purchasing dog carriers, leashes and food bowls at garage sales or go on websites like Craigslist to purchase new pet items for a fraction of what they sell for at retail prices.

WHAT NEVER TO CUT OUT

Invest in your dog's health by maintaining twice-a-year veterinary exams for her. These visits will help your veterinarian catch conditions during their early stages where treatment can be less expensive and there is a greater chance for a full recovery. The sooner problems are detected, the better the prognosis for your dog.

Whittle Down Pet Expenses from the Start

Adopt a dog from your local animal shelter rather than purchasing one from a pet store or breeder. Shelter pets are significantly less expensive, and you are saving an animal's life in the process. Often too, the shelter's nominal adoption fee ensures that your pet has been altered and vaccinated, saving you from these charges at the veterinary clinic.

ENROLL IN A PET FIRST-AID CLASS.

You can learn ways to protect your dog and what to do—and not to do—in a pet emergency when minutes count.

BECOME YOUR DOG'S PERSONAL STYLIST.

Invest in quality nail clippers, brushes and shampoos and learn how to groom, bathe, trim nails and administer flea and tick preventive medicines properly. By regularly grooming your dog, you can prevent hair mats from developing.

Don't Scrimp on Medication

Although some owners might look to save money by giving to their dogs human medications that they already have on hand, veterinarians strongly recommend against it. Many human medications, including acetaminophen, aspirin and ibuprofen, are toxic to dogs. Because dogs metabolize things differently than humans, medications that work for humans won't necessarily work for dogs. On the other hand, low-cost generic medications made for dogs are perfectly fine. Consult your veterinarian.

Pet-proof Your Home

An ounce of accident prevention can save you a lot of money. To reduce the risk of injury-causing accidents, take a good look around your house room by room. Unfortunately, things

Rotate your dog's toys every few days so you don't overbuy the number of toys.

most attractive to dogs can often be the most dangerous. Sidestep a pricey emergency veterinary bill by installing childproof latches (available at your local hardware store) on any drawer or cabinet that contains cleaning supplies, human medication or other items potentially dangerous to your far-too-curious dog. Encase electrical cords in chew-proof PVC tubing. Store kitchen and bathroom trash in containers with sturdy lids with tight seals.

Make Homemade Dog Toys

Got a dog you want to nickname Jaws because she quickly shreds toys you buy at your local pet supply store? You want to provide her with plenty of toys to keep her happy and healthy, but replacing these toys can take a big bite out of your wallet. Instead, save some money by unleashing your creativity by crafting these DIYDTs—that stands for Do It Yourself Dog Toys:

1 Cut holes in a plastic water bottle small enough to dispense kibble when your dog rolls the bottle around.

2 Give your orphaned white athletic sock a second life by placing one of your dog's old tennis balls inside it and pushing it down to the toe. Then, tie a knot just above the ball to seal it inside. Call your dog over for a game of fetch or tug-of-war.

3 Make a nifty dog toy out of a thick braided rope and a tennis ball. Simply cut a hole in the top and bottom of the tennis ball and pull the thick rope through. Then tie knots on the top and bottom of the rope to keep the ball in place—and to give you a good grip during tug-of-war play sessions with your dog. This also doubles as a suitable chew toy for your dog.

Make sure any small items like needles and thread, hair ties, jewelry and coins are out of paw's reach. You don't want the risk of your puppy sniffing and then swallowing these items, which can become entangled in her intestinal tract, causing severe internal damage.

4 Once you finish that plastic bottle of water, remove its cap and slide the empty bottle inside a white athletic sock. Press down to squeeze out the air from the bottle and then knot the top end of the sock. The crackling sound from the plastic bottle and the cottony texture from the sock are double delights of temptation to your play-minded canine.

Pros and Cons of Pet Insurance

The good news: veterinary medicine advances—high-tech tools and disease-fighting medicines—are keeping pets healthy longer. But paying for those advances can take a big bite out of your wallet. Sure, you can dream of winning the lottery, but how financially prepared are you to cover a costly veterinary bill? Where will the money come from? You could use a credit card with high interest rates. Or tap into your dream vacation savings account. Or hope your veterinarian will agree to a monthly payment plan. There's another option: pet insurance. Pet insurance is especially important for pet owners on a budget, where an unexpected expense for their pet could cause them to delay or not seek care for their pet. It's for those who want to offer their pets medical treatments, such as chemotherapy, but can't afford the out-of-pocket costs.

WORLDWIDE PET INSURANCE

How well pet insurance is embraced depends on geography. Only 3 percent of Americans with pets have pet insurance as compared to 25 percent of people with pets in Great Britain and 49 percent in Sweden. The reason appears to be that people in Europe have grown up with pet insurance for generations and it is far more accessible. It's been available in Europe since the late 1940s, whereas pet insurance is relatively new in the United States with the first policy sold in 1982.

Keep in mind that there really is no best pet insurance company. The better question you need to ask is, "Which pet insurance company is the best one to insure my pet?" Finally, recognize if pet insurance really won't benefit your situation—say, if you adopt senior pets or adult pets with special needs or enjoy having a house full of dogs and cats. If you fall into any of those scenarios, your best option may be to dedicate a credit card for pet expenses or talk to your veterinarian before a costly calamity strikes to work out a payment plan option.

ASSESS THE LEVEL OF COVERAGE.
Select a plan based on the coverage it provides and not solely on its price. The least expensive plan may provide the least amount of coverage.

BUY WHEN YOU FIRST GET YOUR DOG.
Don't wait to purchase pet insurance until after your pet gets sick. Some plans do not cover pre-existing conditions.

IT IS EASIER TO DOWNGRADE A POLICY.
Get the best policy you can afford on the front end, because it is easier to downgrade rather than attempt to upgrade as your pet ages. Adding policies such as dental and wellness are more expensive if you delay in obtaining them until your pet hits middle age.

MULTI-PET DISCOUNTS ARE POSSIBLE.
Find out if the company offers discounts for coverage of two or more pets.

PERCENTAGE PLANS ARE BEST.
Since the cost for a veterinary procedure can vary from one veterinary clinic to the next, choose a policy that reimburses based on a percentage of the veterinary bill instead of offering a set amount for a condition.

READ THE FINE PRINT.
Read the fine print in the policy contract. Look for any hidden deductibles, such as not covering exam fees, first-day hospitalization costs, or paying less (higher co-pay) for emergency visits or specialists care.

WHAT IS THE PAYMENT CAP?
Find out ahead of time if the plan carries a payment cap per incident, per year or per the lifetime of the pet.

SEEK SPEEDY REIMBURSEMENT.
Seek a company who provides reimbursement to you quickly, within 7 business days.

Consider enrolling in a pet insurance program when you adopt a dog or start a savings account for him to cover medical costs.

CHAPTER 14

The Senior Years

Ageless Tips for Senior Dogs

The muzzle may be gray. Previous daily leashed runs are now walks. Assistance may be needed to get up on your bed or sofa. For years, your now senior dog has been by your side. Now, he needs your special help.

Old age is not a disease—it is simply a stage in life. If you need further proof, I offer two ageless words for you: Betty White. This nonagenarian actress and animal advocate is enjoying a career revival since reaching her eighties and will forever exemplify the positive way to redefine the golden years for both people and pets.

Detecting aging signs in your dog can be tricky. It's easy to overlook that your senior dog takes longer to fetch a tossed ball or seems to snooze much more even when the television volume is high. But inside your dog's body, a lot of hidden aging is taking place. Metabolism slows down. Bone density lessens. Many senior dogs silently suffer the painful effects of osteoarthritis or have diabetes, heart issues or failing kidneys.

Thanks to advances in veterinary medicine, improved commercial diets and a stronger people-pet connection, our dogs are living longer. And that is to be celebrated. Many of us are sharing our homes—and hearts—with senior pets. In fact, one-third of all dogs are at least 7 years old. Depending on the breed, that equates to senior citizenship status. Here are ways to make those senior years truly golden ones for your doggy pal:

BOOK TWICE-A-YEAR SENIOR WELLNESS VETERINARY EXAMS.

As your dog exits middle age, aging accelerates. Prolong his quality of life and, possibly, catch and treat conditions early by scheduling a senior veterinary exam every 6 months. Recommended senior tests include a thorough physical exam, complete blood count screening, urinalysis, fecal exams, blood-chemistry panel, parasite evaluation and, if warranted, X-rays and an ultrasound. These age-related exams aid your veterinarian in catching conditions possibly at the onset when they can be better treated and often at a financial savings to you.

LOOK FOR AGE-CHANGING CLUES.

Once a week, perform a head-to-tail assessment of your dog. Sniff inside his ears and mouth, palpate his abdomen, and run your fingers through his coat. Alert your veterinarian if you detect foul breath, lumps or nasal discharge.

TURN CHOW TIME INTO A HUNTING ADVENTURE.

Keep your dog's mind sharp by going bowl-less on occasion and hiding pieces of kibble in a room for him to find or stashing kibble inside a food puzzle toy for him to nose or swat out. Recognize that as your dog ages, his nutritional needs also change. After all, your senior dog will have different nutritional needs than when he was a puppy. Work with your veterinarian on a diet that best suits your senior canine's needs.

FLOOR YOUR PET WITH SURE-FOOTED DECOR.

Install rubber mats near feeding stations and rug runners on wood or tile hallways to provide traction and reduce the chance of your dog slipping and falling.

STEP UP THE SNOOZING COMFORT.

Older pets spend more time snoozing—up to 14 hours a day. Treat them to cushioned, egg-crate-type padding beds and pet-safe heating elements to soothe their arthritic joints, especially during cold months.

Pet-Proof Your Home, a Second Time

Life has a way of seeming to repeat itself. This is especially true when your dog hits senior status.

Think back a decade or more ago when you first brought home your then-curious and fearless puppy. Remember how dutifully you made your home safe for him, installing doorway gates and childproof latches on cabinets? It's time to pet-proof your home again, this time with a senior-dog safety theme. Since senior dogs are at increased risk for mobility issues due to arthritis, hip dysplasia or more sores, consider making these easy changes and additions:

- Swap out the old dog beds with orthopedic pet beds designed to cushion joints.
- Turn on pet-safe heating pads set on low settings during cold temperatures to improve blood flow and circulation in their arthritic bodies.
- Ramp it up. Older dogs with arthritis and mobility issues can benefit by learning to use portable steps or ramps to get up onto and down from your sofa and bed.
- Elevate food and water bowls to ward off any neck strain for your senior dog to stay nourished. Replace the deep food bowl with a plate.

Maximize your pet's senior years by clearing the air—literally. If you smoke, stop. Research conducted at leading veterinary universities confirms that there is a direct correlation between people smoking in the home and an increased risk of cancer in their dogs. And more alarming news: More evidence is emerging to verify that thirdhand smoke—the tobacco toxin leftovers that stick on skin, hair, clothing, curtains and household items—can also make their way to your pet's lungs and set the stage for cancer. A fastidious dog grooming his coat is ingesting nicotine and other cigarette toxins with each lick.

Teaching an Old Dog New Tricks

You never want to stop learning and neither do your pets. Once your dog reaches senior status, don't stop purposeful playtime with him. Make it your quest to provide him with age-appropriate environmental enrichments that make his life more fulfilling. And there is a medical benefit to this. The stress of living a boring, monotonous life can contribute to a senior dog becoming stressed and developing urinary tract infections or bladder infections.

If your dog has had a lifelong love of playing tug-of-war with you, select toys of soft materials that won't cause injury to his teeth or gums. If he loves to fetch, switch from tossing the ball to rolling the ball on the ground to prevent him from trying to leap up and possibly pulling a leg muscle. If your grand old dog can no longer walk very far, treat him to the sights and smells of the outdoors by placing him inside a doggy stroller and going for a spin around the neighborhood.

FOOD FOR YOUR SENIOR DOG

Don't be fooled by the label "senior" on commercial dog food packages. There is no legal meaning for senior pet food—it is a marketing term. Instead, work closely with your veterinarian to select food that matches your aging pet's activity level, breed and health condition. For example, some senior dogs may be contending with brain changes that lessen their appetite. Re-spark their interest at mealtime by warming their food in the microwave for a few seconds to release the aroma and/or add salt-free chicken broth to their dry food.

There are many ways to spark an appetite in your aging dog.

Canine Dementia

The good news is that dogs are living longer, with some reaching geriatric status. The sad news is that some dogs, like some people, can develop dementia.

When I adopted Chipper, my Golden Retriever-Husky mix, she was a high-energy 2-year-old in desperate need of guidance and direction. She could sprint down the beach with ease, somehow managing to dodge the sand castles under construction by toddlers. A decade later, she unleashes her energy by making three or four dashes back and forth in my fenced backyard. Then she stops, pants and heads for the water bowl. I notice that her face is much whiter now and there is a bit of glaze in her eyes when the sun hits just right. But for now, she still appears to detect the faintest sounds, smells and sights inside the house and in our neighborhood. I remind myself that each day I get to spend with Chipper is a gift and that she has always been there for me.

But I am very aware that as our beloved pets transition from seniors to geriatrics, they are also susceptible to age-related conditions, including arthritis, diabetes, heart disease and cognitive dysfunction, similar to Alzheimer's disease in people. Cognitive dysfunction (also known as dementia or senility) is a neurological disorder of older dogs characterized by a decline in cognitive ability due to brain aging. Some dogs start to exhibit certain telltale signs of cognitive dysfunction as early as age 9. Veterinary and behavioral experts use the acronym DISH to refer to the symptoms and signs commonly associated with canine senility.

"D" IS FOR DISORIENTED.
Pets who are disoriented often walk aimlessly, stare at walls, or get stuck in corners.

"I" IS FOR INTERACTIONS.
Pets with impaired mental function often become less likely to greet people when they come home or seek out a lap.

"S" IS FOR SLEEP.
Dogs who once slept soundly through the night may prowl or pace restlessly at night and may vocalize as they roam.

"H" IS FOR HOUSETRAINING.

Some dogs suddenly forget their stellar housetraining habits and begin to piddle on the floor instead of alert you that they need to go outside to relieve themselves. If your dog is exhibiting any of these signs, please have your veterinarian perform a thorough examination, which will include blood and urine tests. Your golden oldie may have a physical condition that could be treated with medicine or at least slowed down.

Sadly, there is no cure for cognitive dysfunction in our pets—yet. We can't put the brakes on the number of birthdays our pets accumulate, but we can take purposeful steps to keep them feeling years younger. Veterinary researchers are learning ways to manage senility with memory-improving medications and specially formulated senior diets.

Know When to Say Goodbye

Knowing when to say goodbye to your terminally ill dog is never easy. We love our pets and we do struggle with end-of-life issues. Veterinary associations have created senior care guidelines for dogs and cats. These guidelines identify five "freedoms" to help determine if euthanasia is warranted:

- Freedom from hunger and thirst
- Freedom from physical and thermal discomfort
- Freedom from pain, injury and disease
- Freedom from fear and distress
- Freedom to express normal behavior

Think of four or five things that your dog really likes to do and that give him his personality. Then realize that when those things start to go away, then your dog is also going away mentally and physically. You reach a point where the dog you know is not there anymore. Euthanasia is a gift of love, the last gift you can give your beloved pet.

When it is time to say goodbye to your dear old dog, arrange for a send off that includes family members, including other pets.

Adopting a Senior Dog

Sadly, there are many senior-aged dogs in shelters and at breed rescue sites looking for a second chance at a loving home. You can make a wonderful difference in their lives.

Thinking about adopting a dog or two? Give special consideration to canines who have surpassed their 7th birthdays. By doing so, you save your sanity by skipping the crazy puppyhood time. Let me happily share five reasons to adopt a senior dog:

PREDICTABLE PERSONALITIES.
If you adopt a senior dog who is a sweet dog, you will have a sweet dog when you take him home. The personality has been developed, so there are no surprises. What you see is what you get.

DO NOT DEVIATE IN SIZE OR APPETITE.
Whether you adopted a petite or a gigantic-sized senior dog, you will know exactly how much food you need to buy.

THEY ARE CHAMPIONS OF POWER NAPS.
Puppies possess so much energy and can disrupt your sleep at night. On the other hand, senior dogs are far calmer and enjoy sleeping a lot. You stand a better chance of enjoying a full night's sleep.

THEY ARE MORE MELLOW THAN MISCHIEVOUS.
Puppies and young dogs can be so fearless, so you have to worry more about them ingesting string or other foreign bodies or suffering from a trauma. That's not so much the case with wiser senior dogs.

YOU WILL BE SAVING A LIFE AND MAKING WAY FOR ANOTHER TO WIN A HOME.
When you adopt a senior dog from a shelter, you earn major karma points, in my view. You are also making it possible for the shelter to showcase other strays to help them find homes.

HOW OLD IS YOUR DOG?

Nix the notion that 1 dog year equals 7 human years. It is a myth without merit. The truth is that the true age of a dog (in human years) is based on his weight. Small dogs tend to age slower than giant breeds. This chart provides an accurate comparison based on a dog's weight.

DOG'S AGE	UNDER 20 lbs	21–50 lbs	51–90 lbs	91–PLUS lbs
1	15	15	15	15
2	24	24	24	24
3	28	28	28	28
4	32	32	34	36
5	36	36	40	42
6	40	42	45	49
7	44	47	50	56
8	48	51	55	64
9	52	56	61	71
10	56	60	66	78
11	60	65	72	86
12	64	69	77	93
13	68	74	82	101
14	72	78	88	108
15	76	83	93	115
16	80	87	99	123
17	84	92	104	—
18	88	96	109	—
19	92	101	115	—

If you have a small dog and a large dog who are both 13, take note of how much older your larger dog is in terms of human years.

Further Reading

BOOKS BY ARDEN MOORE:

🐾 *What Dogs Want: A Visual Guide to Understanding Your Dog's Every Move*
Firefly Books Ltd, 2012

🐾 *The Dog Behavior Answer Book*
Storey Books, 2006

🐾 *Happy Dog, Happy You*
Storey Publishing, 2008

🐾 *Real Food for Dogs*
Storey Publishing, 2003

🐾 *Healthy Dog: The Ultimate Fitness Guide for You and Your Dog*
BowTie Press, 2004

🐾 *Dog Parties: How to Party with Your Pup*
i5 Press, 2004

🐾 *Dog Training: A Lifelong Guide*
i5 Press, 2002

BOOKS RECOMMENDED BY AUTHOR ARDEN MOORE:

🐾 *Good Old Dog*
by the faculty of Cummings School of Veterinary Medicine at Tufts University
Houghton Mifflin Harcourt, 2010

🐾 *Chow Hounds: Why Our Dogs Are Getting Fatter* by Ernie Ward, DVM
HCI, 2010

🐾 *30 Days to a Well-Mannered Dog*
by Tamar Gellar
Gallery Books 2011

🐾 *Your Dog: The Owner's Manual*
by Marty Becker, DVM
Grand Central Life & Style 2012

🐾 *How to Behave So Your Dog Behaves*
by Sophia Yin, DVM
TFH Publications, 2010

🐾 *Train Your Dog Positively*
by Victoria Stilwell
Ten Speed Press 2013

🐾 *How to Speak Dog* by Aline Alexander Newman and Gary Weitzman, DVM
National Geographic Children's Books, 2013

ABOUT ARDEN MOORE:

Arden Moore—The Pawsitive Coach™—happily wears many "collars" in the pet world: radio show host, author, professional speaker, editor, media consultant, dog/cat behavior consultant and master pet first-aid instructor. Each week, more than one million people tune into her *Oh Behave Show* on Pet Life Radio, the world's No. 1 pet radio network. Arden's guests include A-list celebrities and "top dogs" in the pet industry.

Arden is the founder of Four Legged Life, an online pet community, and creator of National Dog Party Day, an annual event that raises money for pet charities and brings out the playful party animal in people and their dogs. As an in-demand pet safety, behavior and lifestyle expert, Arden is on a mission: to bring out the best in pets and their people. She shares her home with two dogs, two cats and an overworked vacuum cleaner. Learn more at www.fourleggedlife.com.

Index

Picture Credits